Echoes in the Air

Echoes in the Air

A chronicle of aeronautical ghost stories

by Jack Currie

Crécy Publishing Limited

Echoes in the Air
Volume 1

Published in 1998
by Crécy Publishing Limited

ISBN 0 947554 742

Crécy Publishing Limited
1a, Ringway Trading Estate, Shadowmoss Road,
Manchester M22 5LH

Illustration Acknowledgments

Cover Mark Smith

Prelude

X Via Kate Currie
  (Garbett/Goulding)
XII Mark Smith
XV Mark Smith

Ripples in the Atmosphere

1 Mark Smith
2 RAF Museum, 5928-1
3 Mark Smith
4 Mark Smith
5 Mark Smith
6 Mark Smith
7 Mark Smith
8 Mark Smith
9 Mark Smith
10 Mark Smith

The Polish Airman

11 Mark Smith
12 Mark Smith
13 RAF Museum, P017880
14 Quadrant Picture Library
  (Flight Magazine)
15 Lynn Williams
16 Quadrant Picture Library
  (Flight Magazine)
17 Mark Smith
18 RAF Museum, P017884
20 Mark Smith

Cold Over Heligoland

21 Via Kate Currie
23 Quadrant Picture Library
  (Flight Magazine)
24 John M Dibbs
26 Lynn Williams
28 RAF Museum, P017881
30 Lynn Williams
31 Military Aircraft
  Photographs
32 Lynn Williams

The Montrose Ghost and Others

33 RAF Museum, P6993
34 Left - RAF Museum
34 Right - Quadrant Picture
  Library (Flight Magazine)
35 Left - Quadrant Picture
  Library (Flight Magazine)
35 Top Right - RAF Museum,
  P517
35 Middle Right - Quadrant
  Picture Library (Flight
  Magazine)
36 RAF Museum, P016959
37 Mark Smith
38 RAF Museum, P017716
39 RAF Museum, 5968-9
40 Mark Smith
42 Mark Smith
43 Top - Mark Smith
43 Middle - DF Daniells,

by kind permission of
Mr J R Hildreth
43 Bottom - DF Daniells,
  courtesy of the Microlight
  Flying School, Rufforth
44 DF Daniells
45 Quadrant Picture Library
  (Flight Magazine)

Flight 401

47 Quadrant Picture Library
  (Flight Magazine)
49 Quadrant Picture Library
  (Flight Magazine)
50 Lynn Williams
52 Quadrant Picture Library
  (Flight Magazine)
54 Quadrant Picture Library
  (Flight Magazine)

The Watch Tower

55 Mark Smith
56 Mark Smith
57 via Wallace R. Forman
58 Mark Smith
60 Mark Smith
61 Mark Smith
62 Mark Smith

The Legends of North Weald

63 Military Aircraft
  Photographs
64 Jeremy M Pratt

Contents

Prelude

Jeremy M Pratt – Publisher

From the first floor of the control tower I had a commanding view across the old airfield. Two of the runways crossed directly ahead of the control tower windows, and stretched down to a minor road that cut directly across the site. This small corner of the airfield was still – supposedly – used by light aircraft, whilst on the far side of the road the disused portion of the two runways, and the mile-long concrete strip that had once been the main runway, was slowly turning back to farmland. Crumbling taxyways and abandoned dispersals marked the perimeter track, its protective loop now broken and decaying. Behind the control tower was a small cluster of hangars, which ought to contain some sort of human activity, but like the rest of the airfield seemed to be devoid of any life whatsoever. Beyond the hangars were the woods, and the odd glimpse of overgrown huts, long deserted. My eyes roved across this tableau and, in all of this, I was all alone: a single human observer on this desolate aerodrome, this field of ghosts.

Beyond the aerodrome boundary lay the flat Lincolnshire fields and, just visible to the south, the mighty spire of Lincoln Cathedral rose above this vista, as majestic as the masts of a sailing ship on a distant ocean horizon. Nothing stirred save the wind, whipping across the landscape, plucking the dying autumn leaves from the trees and hedges and pushing them into corners and doorways, or twisting them into a merry dance that briefly pirouetted across the broken concrete before collapsing in an exhausted heap. Cloud shadows raced across the airfield and the sun, already low in its arc, lit the floating dust behind the windows of the control tower in auburn shafts of light. Except for the wind pushing through the gaps in the ancient window frames, the ticking of the wall clock and the hiss of static from an unattended radio, there was silence. How many before me had stood on this spot and looked out from these windows? What mortal struggles, what dreams and despairs had been witnessed from here? Had great endeavours shaped this place, only to become forgotten and neglected as the years passed? How long I stood there, lost in these thoughts, I do not know. But when a voice spoke out, its owner having ascended the stairs behind me unseen and unheard, I started as if 10,000 volts had been passed through me, my heart racing and the metallic taste of adrenaline in my mouth. I was lost for a moment, the reverie broken, until I found my bearings and gathered my senses.

Later, much later, I was to read of another person's first impressions of this very place, gained more than 40 years earlier when it played its part in a great life and death struggle for survival between nations – the Second World War. The watch tower (as it was then known), the hangars and the runways were the same, but the scene could not have been more different:

Behind the watch tower, among the drab stone and iron buildings, a crew bus was leaving the locker-room. It turned on to the perimeter track and drove off towards the dispersal pans on my left. Another crew bus was filling up, a group of men wearing life-jackets and parachute harnesses passed ration boxes, navigation bags. flying-jackets and parachutes to those inside. The small figure of a red-haired WAAF driver stood by the double doors, helping the encumbered crews aboard.

A motor-bicycle appeared among the trees, threaded a way through the crowd outside the locker-room, and accelerated across the perimeter track. Gravel scraped as the rider braked under the watch-tower windows, and the motor stammered and stopped as he pulled the cut-out. I watched the rider tugging off his gauntlets and entering the tower, glancing over his shoulder at the darkening eastern sky. As I followed the direction of his glance, I caught the movement I had been awaiting on the dispersals to my right. The port outer propellers of two neighbouring bombers were slowly turning, and, as I watched, a blue-grey plume of smoke curled from the exhaust of the nearer aircraft, the propeller-blades turned faster and blurred into invisibility. A second later the sound of the engine reached me, roaring harshly as it started, then settling to a heavy drone. The port inner engine fired in turn, followed by the starboard inner, starboard outer, and now from dispersals all around the airfield came initial roar and subsequent rumble as the bombers came to life.

A small fleet of vehicles was assembling beside the watch-tower: fire tenders, two flight vans, an ambulance and a Hillman saloon flying a pennant on the bonnet which I took to identify the Station Commander. Other vehicles were moving on the perimeter track between dispersals, but even those that passed me closely were soundless against the growing clamour of the aircraft engines...

Now all around the darkening airfield the bombers were moving, making the amber taxiway lamps twinkle as they passed between them, forming two processions, one from either side of the main runway, converging on the steady red light that marked the airfield controller's caravan. Between the two processions glowed the flarepath lights.

A green light flickered from the caravan - the leading aircraft moved on to the runway, straightened into wind, paused while the engines cleared their throats, and drove, uncertainly at first and then with gathering momentum, into headlong chase for flight. As it lifted, the next Lancaster was already rolling forward, and then another, until three aircraft moved within my field of vision. The first was slowly climbing to the left, its navigation lights just visible above the tree line, the second running tail-up for take-off, and the third swinging on to the runway by the caravan. The air was becoming filled with heavy noise, which mounted to a peak as each successive bomber passed my vantage point. I put my fingers to my ears, and wondered how much noise the night could hold.

It must have been some six hours later that the first returning bomber wakened me, and I lay in the dark hut listening to the change of key as the airscrews sped to overcome the added drag of the main wheels thrusting from their housings. Then the sound was multiplied as other bombers joined the circuit, and soon the reverberation of *their growling engines lulled me back to sleep.*

As I left the airfield on an autumn day four decades later, I knew nothing of this past. I knew only that there was an atmosphere here, a sense that this place, and especially the old watch tower, was the guardian of untold secrets, a memorial to great deeds. I returned more than once, and each time I was touched by the same ambience I had encountered on my first visit. In time I learnt more about these old airfields, about the courageous deeds they witnessed, about the cost in young human lives. I began to wonder if these events could leave intangible traces that were more than physical, some kind of resonance, an echo maybe. Like most pilots I heard many a story, usually told in an airfield bar, about the ghosts of aircrew, possessed hangars and haunted control towers, ghostly bombers returning to their old bases, premonitions and inexplicable co-incidences. Many of these accounts could be dismissed as fanciful, but even a cynic had to wonder what truth there might be in some of these tales.

An unexpected turn of events led me to take on a small publishing company. The notion of a book about the ghosts of the air had grown within me, and I put the idea to one of our authors, Jack Currie, himself a former wartime bomber pilot. To my delight he accepted the commission and, as the reader will find, he accomplished the task with skill and dedication. We already published four of Jack's

books, and there was talk of more books to follow, but it was not to be. On the 19th October 1996 Jack Currie passed away, after a courageous fight against one final enemy. In a quiet Yorkshire churchyard he was laid to rest before a multitude of friends, family and former colleagues. Later, a flight of RAF Tucanos provided an airborne salute over his home.

I took the decision to complete 'Echoes in the Air', in the way that I believe he would have done himself. There was so much material that I decided to publish the work in two volumes. I have selected the stories for this first part, and also added two further chapters, 'Turn Back, Turn Back' and 'Captain Black' that arrived too late for Jack to work on. I have credited the writer of each in the relevant chapter. In addition, new information has come to light, certain facts have been verified or corrected, photographs have been procured. Inevitably, I have made a few minor changes to maintain the accuracy of the text, but in doing so I have been careful to preserve what I see as the spirit and intent of Jack's words. When he wrote to me, sometimes to deliver a reprimand for an error or omission (as authors are wont to do to publishers), Jack's letters would often close with the admonishment that I must "Straighten up and fly right". In completing this book, I have done my best to do just that; not least because, as Jack himself describes in the epilogue to this book, those involved in the book – especially the deceased – have found their own ways to make their feelings known.

Back on that autumn day when I looked out across an old airfield, I could not have imagined what my thoughts and impressions would lead to. With hindsight, it seems stranger still. The airfield is called Wickenby, it was home to Lancaster bombers during the Second World War. The passage describing a bomber raid setting out from there in 1943 comes from one of the classic books about life in Bomber Command – *Lancaster Target*, subtitled 'The story of a crew who flew from Wickenby'; a book which launched the writing career of its author. It is a book of which I knew nothing until nearly a decade after I first stood in that deserted control tower.

Lancaster Target was written by Jack Currie.

The signals square next to the control tower.
Wickenby, 1996

Ripples in the Atmosphere

To begin with, let me try to establish the premises on which this book is written, and to explain what I mean when I use the word "ghost". First, I hope the reader will accept that there are some happenings in life that can neither be classified as illusory nor as undisputed fact: they seem to lie somewhere in-between. We hear from time to time of extraordinary occurrences, any one of which would be dismissed by most of us as a piece of fantasy, or at best as the product of imagination, but which are nonetheless real enough to the people who witness them. The lives of quite normal, ordinary people are sometimes touched by strange, inexplicable encounters, usually connected with something that happened in the past. It may be that some occurrences do not answer to a normal time scale, that they are set in a different dimension and have a different frequency, that they evoke a sort of ripple in the atmosphere which tends to linger on – a continuing echo of a past event.

Secondly, to clarify the terms, what I take a ghost to be is a dead person appearing to the living, and words like "phantom", "spectre" and "apparition" I take to be synonymous. I do not argue with the view that no-one really dies, that we merely "shuffle off this mortal coil" and continue an existence on a different plane, and maybe several different planes, but for this book's purposes, "dead" means physically extinct. From all that I can gather, there are two main varieties of ghost. There are those of souls who died in the normal way of things, either due to illness or simply from using up their life-span, as we understand it. Such ghosts appear but rarely, usually to a close relative or friend, seldom more than once, and their visitations tend to remain unknown outside the family circle. The others, the ones we are more likely to hear about, are the ghosts of men or women whose lives ended suddenly, untimely and violently, with their hopes and dreams remaining unfulfilled. Their deaths are often due to murder, execution, or to act of war, and these are the ghosts that continue to appear, however intermittently, usually near the places where they died, or where they were taken from to die. In other words, they haunt, and if you happen to be at one of those locations, and to be on the right wave-length at the right time, they may reveal themselves to you, or in some way let you know that they are there.

All the stories in this book are in one way or another related to the air – to aircraft and fliers, the airfields that they flew from, and sometimes to the effects they have had on people's lives. The material comes from various sources: firstly, from my own interest in, and study of, the subject of flight, and all the phenomena, sometimes very strange, which go along with that; secondly, from the volume of responses evoked by the requests I placed in a few appropriate magazines and journals. Thirdly, I was lucky in obtaining the assistance of David Bannister of Warboys, a village in what used to be Huntingdonshire and is now part of Cambridgeshire. The village gave its name to the nearby RAF airfield where, from 1942 to 1945, the Pathfinder crews of No. 8 Group were trained, especially in the navigation skills they needed for the special task of finding and illuminating targets for the heavy bombers. Nurtured in this area, in the midst of a cluster of old airfields, David has taken a strong interest in the air war, and is an honourary member of the Pathfinder Association.

In compiling the stories from each of these sources, certain patterns have emerged. Ghosts, for example, whether of airmen or of anybody else, as they are reported, do not often speak, and very seldom touch; they do not shriek and gibber, they do not prance about, bathed in unearthly light and wearing burial shrouds; they are not aggressive, nor do they pose a threat. The few that are reported to have spoken seem to have done so quietly and obliquely, not always apropos of what is going on, and that seems understandable and logical – if such a term is not unsuited to the context – because whatever needs and motivations they may have are on a different plane from ours, and of a different sort. In some appearances by ghosts, as they have been described by a witness or witnesses, they emerge out of a sort of cloud, which first becomes a halo or a cloudy outline, and then

disappears, leaving the ghost's face or figure either perfectly clear – so clear that it seems entirely natural and real – or a little blurred, like a photograph slightly out of focus, or like a television picture when there is some static interference or the reception is a little off frequency.

According to the expert, Tony Ellis of Smethwick, who has made a life-long study of psychical phenomena, these apparitions are caught in a "time maze", or as some would say in limbo, hovering between this life and whatever follows. "In the majority of cases," Ellis says, "they are unaware that they are being witnessed as they stroll down memory lane, and if they are disturbed, they quickly disappear." That may well be so, but it is also possible that some are searching for the password, for the formula or key that will admit them to the future state, and that they need our assistance in their quest.

In the future state, whatever or wherever it may be, Ellis is convinced from his experience that communication with the living can exist, but for the majority of people, including me, the concept of talking and being talked to by the dead, albeit through a medium on one side and some kind of mystic contact on the other, is weird, if not to say fantastic. And yet, it seems to happen. Thousands

of intelligent, educated men and women are entirely sure of it, it illuminates their lives, and it continues to go on, through all sorts of channels – the mind of a trance-medium, by automatic writing, the use of a Ouija board, or simple table-tapping. Somewhere, at this moment, as the reader scans this page, people are believing that they are in contact with a relative or friend whose bones lie underground, or whose ashes have been scattered to the winds.

Some of those people may be victims of a clever trick, or of an illusion; some, on the other hand, may not. For them, it will be a real experience, like talking on the telephone to a person in another part of England, or another country. The difference is that the normal vocabulary of life on earth will not quite meet the case. Here, we establish relationships in terms of place, time and circumstance, by discussing our affairs, our hobbies and often the weather. Away from here, those parameters, those pursuits, have no related context. "There" and "here" seem to have lost their meaning, as do "when" and "where".

The difficulty lies in persuading the imagination to make the quantum leap that is required. Seeing is

believing, and it is hard, if not impossible, to form a picture of "the other side" – of where those dead souls are, of how they look or what they wear; do they sit, stand, or somehow float? What is the geography? We are accustomed to accepting voices from the air, voices on the radio and on the telephone, but then we know, and can visualise, that a solid person is doing the talking. What is hard to accept is a disembodied voice from out of nowhere, because the basic, earthly questions keep arising, of how they do it, how can it be possible? Unless we can accept that some phenomena are outside our range, beyond our understanding, we cannot come to terms with the supernatural, nor is there any reason why we should, unless we feel the need and are willing to explore. Very well, we may say, an interest in seances, spiritualism and psychic exploration does no-one any harm, and if it makes people happy, good for them, and we should not decry it. It may not be for us, but who knows that it might be, at some time in the future? Perhaps we ought not to assume that the sort of physical space we know is not the only sort there is, nor that the measurements of time which rule all our earthly lives hold equal sway beyond life.

There are people, and perhaps they are the realists (sometimes known as humanists), who believe that when you die, there is an end of it – *finito la commedia* – and there are those, the orthodox religionists, who hold that there is a life hereafter, in another, better place. One thing is certain – no-one really knows. At this point, the reader may feel inclined to ask if I have ever seen a

ghost, and the answer is, I have. But one of my experiences had nothing to do with flying or the air, so it does not fall within the province of this book; I shall recount the others in later chapters. Meanwhile, I take my stance beside the lady who, when asked if she believed in ghosts, replied after due consideration that, on the whole, she thought appearances were in their favour.

A lot of strange stories emanate from England's eastern counties – from the flat lands north of London, from East Anglia and Lincolnshire, and the broad Yorkshire plains – the regions of this country where the Royal Air Force and the United States Army Air Force based their heavy bombers. There are stories of a phantom Lancaster, bearing the code letters "PM" of No.103 Squadron on its fuselage, roaring off into the twilight, from Elsham Wolds in Lincolnshire, forty years after the airfield had been closed; people hear the sound of engines in an empty hangar at North Pickenham in Norfolk; many feel a chilling presence in the watch-tower at Thorpe Abbotts, home of the USAAF's 100th Bomb Group – known as the "Bloody Hundredth" for its heavy casualty roll; a voice is often heard at Tibenham, the Norfolk base of the 445th Bomb Group's Liberators, rapping out orders through a non-existent Tannoy, accompanied by the roar as a pilot checks his engines at full power, rattling the windows and the crockery in what is now a glider clubhouse.

Many folk have heard the growl of heavy aircraft returning in the morning to a long-deserted base; flying control at Waddington in 1948 received signals from an unseen Lancaster using voice and Morse code call-signs that had last been current in 1943; night travellers in North Lincolnshire have seen a flarepath burning in the meadows where an airfield used to be; a group of airmen have been witnessed, walking on a path that was only there in wartime, and passing through a wall that was built in recent years; there have been sounds of conversation in what used to be a crew-room, of a piano playing without a pianist in an officers' mess ante-room,

of activity and laughter in what was once a squash court; at a wartime bomber base, now a training school, a tall, shadowy figure passes silently through the corridors of the flying control tower; old photographs of aircrews fall unaided off the wall in the "The Blacksmith's Arms", No. 10 Squadron's favourite pub near Melbourne, now renamed the "Bombers"; the site of the old Nissen huts at Leconfield is haunted by a figure who wears a flying helmet, but is without a face…

Before concluding this introductory chapter, I should assure readers that they need have no qualms about letting their children read any portion of this book, nor need the most delicately-nurtured fear that any story in it might disturb their dreams. There will be no shroud-wrapped skeletons, no empty, glaring eye-sockets and no fleshless, gaping mouths. Such ghoulish images lie in the realm of fiction, and have no place in what is intended to be a serious exploration of the subject.

It must also be said that there will be no reference to reported sightings of the spirits either of Wing Commander Guy Gibson of the RAF, or of Major Glenn Miller of the USAAF. It is not that I disbelieve all such reports, but my feeling is they stem largely from illusions that are self-induced and, intriguing as they may be, I do not find them totally convincing. And because there are so many, I shall not dwell at any length on accounts from people who believe that they have

felt a drop in temperature, or sensed an unseen presence, on visits to disused airfields. Further, there will be no reference to Unidentified Flying Objects because, for one thing, they do not seem to lie within the spirit field, and for another, I have never seen one. These limitations stated, it is time to embark on the first, and what must be one of the best documented, ghost stories of the air.

Hatfield Waste, 1996

The Polish Airman

As was suggested in the first chapter, it often seems to be the way with paranormal sights and sounds that they occur at places where people have died suddenly: historic battlefields, the sites of ancient massacres, gallows grounds – and wartime airfields. Certainly, sudden death was commonplace for the young men of the British Empire and Commonwealth and of America, and for the free forces of their European allies, who flew and fought from Britain in the war against the Axis powers. Sometimes, visitors to these locations have experienced a feeling of great sadness, even of despair; given the physical and mental associations, that is understandable. It is notable, however, in the strange anthology of airfield apparitions, that not one of them has appeared to be malevolent: no greater harm than a momentary frightening and a lasting memory has befallen any witness. Well-established phantoms have even come to be regarded with some familiarity, if not to say irreverence, and the following story of the phantom Polish airman at Lindholme is a case in point.

The RAF station at Lindholme was built on four hundred acres of South Yorkshire, on the edge of a peat bog known as Hatfield Waste. When the work began in May 1938, the station was known as Hatfield Woodhouse – the name of the nearest village – and it was to be one of the RAF's first big bomber bases, with five type C1 hangars, a technical site on the southern boundary of the grass airfield, backed by workshops and living accommodation. Construction was delayed for a while when some of the labourers refused to work on a hangar which was to be erected on the west side of the airfield where, admittedly, the atmosphere was peculiarly miasmic and forbidding (nor had it changed when I was serving there in the 1950s). When construction was completed, it was decided that Hatfield Woodhouse was too much of a mouthful for using on RT, there was also a danger of confusion with Hatfield, an existing airfield in Hertfordshire, and it was therefore as RAF Lindholme that the station opened for business in June 1940. On the night of 25/26th August, No. 50 Squadron's aircraft took part in the RAF's first ever mission to Berlin – an attack ordered by Winston Churchill by way of a reprisal for the Luftwaffe's opening air-raid on London. The aircraft were Handley-Page Hampdens, and their fuel tanks had to be topped up at an airfield on the Norfolk coast to enable them to reach the target. They did no great

A Wellington IC (Z1112) of 304 squadron

damage, but at least they got there – Reichsmarschall Hermann Goering, commanding the Luftwaffe, had said they never would.

When No. 50 Squadron was transferred to Swinderby in July 1941, Nos. 304 and 305 Polish squadrons moved in at Lindholme, operating the Vickers Wellington, known as the Wimpey to the RAF. Most of the crewmen had escaped from eastern Europe to carry on the fight, leaving their homes and families behind. Their strong purpose was to kill as many Germans (and, when time permitted, to love as many women) as they could. Some of the pilots had been in the Polish cavalry, and they tended to regard the Wellington as a sort of flying horse, forever at the gallop, if not on the charge. Their morale was always high, and it was raised even higher in April 1942, when they were visited by General Sikorski, their Prime Minister in exile and Commander-in-Chief. With Barnes Wallis's revolutionary geodetic structure, the Wellington could take a lot of punishment, and often had to do so from the flak guns of the Ruhr and other German conurbations. Sometimes, they came back to their airfields full of holes, and it was in such a condition that one of No. 305 Squadron's

aircraft came back to Lindholme from an attack upon Cologne. It overshot the runway, crashed into the bog, and sank out of sight. None of the crew was found, but, shortly afterwards, a number of station personnel reported being approached by a figure, dressed in stained flying kit, who asked for directions to the sick bay in a foreign accent, and, when so directed, promptly disappeared.

In 1944, when Lindholme had become a Heavy Conversion training unit, members of an embryo aircrew, practising "circuits and bumps", observed the distinctive tail and fuselage of a Wellington, breaking the surface of the bog and sinking down again. The aircraft continued to lie there, occasionally emerging, according to some when the moon was full, and to others (more prosaic) when the methane gas in the fuselage had expanded enough to make it rise. The local belief was that, on those occasions, one of the crew also emerged to roam the environs of the base, seeking directions, sometimes to the mess, sometimes to the operations room, and sometimes to the sick bay. Soon, the legend of "Lindholme Willie" or, as others called him, "Pete the Pole", was established .

By 1947, the ghost seemed to have become sufficiently emboldened to appear at billet doors, still asking for directions in the same strange accent. On one occasion, he called the guardroom on the telephone, and the call was traced to that same western hangar where the pre-war construction gangs had refused to work. RAF policemen, checking out the hangar, could not persuade their Alsatian dogs to approach the place. When they surrounded it and entered, leaving the nervous animals outside, they found no-one there.

The 'geodetic' fuselage structure of the Wellington

Not long afterwards, as night flying was finishing out on the airfield, the duty runway controller was startled by the sight of a stained, pale-faced figure tapping on the window of his caravan. This story was still current years later when, as reported by "Peterborough" in The Daily Telegraph: "... at dusk in the winter of 1969 a pilot ejected from his jet after take-off and landed in the bog. He finally reached the airfield and peered in through the window of the lonely caravan occupied by the runway controller. The controller took one look at the pilot's face, screamed and set off up the runway faster than any accelerating jet."

In 1953, when Lindholme had become the RAF's bombing school, Reg Cliffe was a corporal

armourer serving on the squadron I was then commanding, and as such he flew with me on an air show at nearby Finningley, firing smoke cartridges from an Avro Lincoln bomber (the Lancaster's successor) to simulate anti-aircraft fire for the entertainment of the crowd. Over thirty years later, having seen me working on TV, he revealed his memories of "Lindholme Willie". Cliffe had completed his duties in the early morning hours and returned to the ordnance office, which was located in that haunted hangar. "I sent one of the other armourers," he said, "to check that the main hangar door was locked. He was older than us, about thirty, an ex-miner from Newcastle and a quiet, stable sort of chap. Within minutes he was back, as white as a sheet and trembling like a leaf. He said 'I've seen him', and described a figure in a flying suit with a helmet and lifejacket. I know he wasn't acting, he wasn't the type, he just wanted to lock up and get off to bed. After that nobody ever went alone to lock that door after dark."

One year after the armourer's experience, an instrument mechanic, working in the cockpit of one of my squadron's Lincolns in the late evening, saw a shadowed figure approaching the dispersal pan. The mechanic put his head out of the cabin window, and the figure made a gesture indicating eating. "Do you want the mess?" the mechanic called, "Officers or Sarn'ts?" The figure tapped the sleeve of his clothing, indicating non-commissioned rank. "You want to go round the peri-track, Sarge," said the mechanic, "turn left at flying control, and straight on between the hangars." With that, he turned back to the instrument panel and continued with his work.

Squadron aircrew, and their Avro Lincolns.
Lindholme, 1946

On returning to the flight hut, he mentioned the incident to his NCO and described the figure's clothing. "That's a Sidcot suit," the sergeant said. "Aircrew haven't worn Sidcots since the war. You've seen Lindholme Willie, my lad." Unable to put the matter out of mind, the mechanic could not sleep that night. He was late for duty in the morning, his Corporal put him "on a fizzer", and he was duly marched into my office. Intrigued by his story, I delivered a homily and dismissed the charge. The Corporal was somewhat disappointed, and clearly thought me rather gullible.

In the following year, Lindholme Willie succeeded in awakening an entire barrack block full of airmen when, on seeing the helmeted figure bathed in moonlight at his bedside early in the morning, the occupant was moved to let out a series of piercing screams.

Since those sightings, the phantom crewman has appeared to many different witnesses. On an evening in 1960, the Commanding Officer, Group Captain L.D. Mavor (later Air Marshal Sir Leslie), was in his quarters, dressing for a dining-in night in the mess. His wife entered the bedroom, and stood beside him, chatting, as he made up his tie. When the Group Captain turned away, Mrs. Mavor was still looking in the mirror, and she saw the phantom figure clearly, standing behind her at the bedroom door.

The Wellington was eventually recovered from Hatfield Waste in the early 1970s, and the remains of four airmen were buried in the local cemetery. The fifth crew member's body was not found. In 1975, shortly after Lindholme ceased to be an active airfield, Lieutenant-Colonel Stephen Jenkins of Wisbech, a Territorial Army officer, was attending an annual training course at RAF Finningley, some five miles south of Lindholme on the Thorne-Bawtry road. During the night exercise, some of which took place on the edge of Hatfield Waste, Jenkins and an RAF Squadron Leader saw a figure, dressed in flying kit, standing near the spot where

A 305 squadron crew at Lindholme, 1942

the Wellington had sunk. "As we watched," said Jenkins, "the figure disappeared – but it did so where it stood, not by walking away".

In 1985, the Home Office bought the base at Lindholme from the Ministry of Defence for the sum of £17,500,000, and it became one of HM Prisons, category "C". The late Frank Pritchard of Benfleet, Essex, who, as it happened, had also flown with me at Lindholme many years ago, informed me only a few weeks before he died that the phantom had made several visits to the cells. It was Frank's opinion that the occasional escapes by convicts were motivated, less by the natural desire for freedom, than by fear of Lindholme Willie.

The haunted hangar was converted to an agricultural store and the contractor responsible for the work complained of being pestered by a figure dressed in flying clothing and speaking in a foreign tongue. That was the last known visitation: on 23rd July 1987, forty-six years to the day after the Polish Squadrons' first foray from Lindholme, a Fisons workman, employed on digging peat, found the well-preserved body of a young Polish airman, whose injuries were consistent with a fall from height. Identification proved to be impossible and, at 11 a.m. on 11th November 1987, the body was buried in the cemetery at RAF Finningley, the nearest active airfield at that time. No more wanderings, no more need for sustenance or medical attention. Rest in peace, young Polish airman.

The grave of the unknown Polish airman at Finningley

Jack Currie's crew
(minus Jim Cassidy, who was at a briefing).
Left to right Larry Myring, Jack Currie, Len Bretell, George Protheroe, Johnny Walker, Charlie Fairburn

Cold Over Heligoland

The following stories are concerned with the inexplicable behaviour of five different aeroplanes. The first, from which the chapter takes its name, describes an experience of my own. Had it not occurred, the chances are that what remained of my bones would still be resting on the bottom of the cold North Sea.

The weather over Hamburg on the night of 2nd/3rd August 1943 was the nastiest I, for one, had ever known, and in another twenty years of flying, I never met weather quite so bad again. It was the fourth night in a series of attacks during which our commander, Air Chief Marshal Harris, intended to destroy the enemy's second city and main port. During the second attack, on the night of 27th July, hundreds of fires had been started in the city, and these, aided by unusually hot, dry conditions on the ground, had merged together to create a fire-storm. The fire services had been overwhelmed, tens of thousands had died, and two-thirds of the surviving population had been evacuated by the time the third attack went in two nights later.

I suppose it is possible that if the extent of devastation had been known at the time, the fourth and last attack would never have been mounted, but great palls of smoke hid Hamburg from the recce aircraft, and we at Wickenby, along with another 700 bombers, had been briefed to go again. We were told that an active cold front was expected over the North Sea, but that once we got through that the skies above the target should be clear. As sometimes happened, that was not quite the way it was. Tonight, it seemed that Mother Nature had taken Hamburg under her protection, and had thrown a shield around the city – a great barrier of thunder cloud, towering to 30,000 feet, full of violent turbulence and ice.

Approaching the target at 19,000 feet, B-Baker Two's thirty tons had been tossed up and down like a toy boat in a maelstrom; the port outer engine stopped, and the navigator's radar followed suit. If there had been any target marker-flares, nobody could have seen them. I told Larry Myring to let the bombs go down, if only because there was nothing else to do with them, but as to where they landed, we could only tell that it was somewhere in the environs of the port.

Turning for home, I tried all I knew to find a pathway through the savage clouds, all garishly illumined by jagged lightning flashes, but each way I turned, another great anvil-top loomed ahead. Baker Two felt intolerably heavy and she was losing height, although her airspeed was only just above the stall. I had got a taste of how it felt to be frightened on two trips to Cologne, and I knew better than to let it put me off – I just kept trying to "straighten up and fly right", the way I had been taught.

The flak bursts came up, one after another, right on track. Instinctively, I swung the nose away, and flew straight into one of those towering clouds. Almost at once, the controls froze up completely, and I was just sitting there, unable to push or pull the column, turn the spectacles or move the rudder bars. I watched the St. Elmo's fire dancing round the front guns and the windshield, saw the ice shining on the wings, and heard the solid chunks of it flying off the prop blades and smashing on the fuselage. A sudden up-current seized us, the straps of the safety harness bit into my shoulders, and I knew we had turned over.

The nose sank and we were falling, down through the chasms of the cloud, with vivid streaks of lightning all around us. It was an eerie sight. I looked away from it, and tried to make some sense out of the instruments. They were of little help: the altimeter was unwinding at a rapid rate, the airspeed indicator needle was fast against its stop at 410 MPH (360 was supposed to be the limit), the turn and slip needles were in the corners of the dial, and the little gyro compass was spinning round and round. I switched the mike on and told the crew "Parachutes on, prepare to jump".

Later, I realised that all through the spin, I had been trying to do the things I had learned to do a year ago, in the clear, blue skies of Georgia: full opposite rudder, regain lateral control and ease out of the dive. The trouble was that none of the controls would move, although I must have kept on trying all the time. Meanwhile, I was trying to decide what height I would tell the crew to jump. It would have to be soon, because we were going down so fast. It was then that I felt a sudden violent jerk on the spectacles, followed by another; then they went slack, and I knew that something nasty had happened to the ailerons. Almost immediately, Baker Two shot out of the cloud base and into the clear. She had spun, dived and tumbled through 10,000 feet, but she had survived. Some aeroplane, the Lancaster.

I didn't need the mid-upper gunner's shocked report that both the ailerons were missing ("bloody great chunks out of the wings", was how he chose to put it) – I knew that from the feel of the controls. I still had the rudders, the elevators and the power of all the engines (the dead one had come to life when we broke out of the cloud). The crew resumed their stations, all except for the flight engineer, who had been dropping "window" through the flare-chute when the aeroplane turned over, had hit a metal member with his head and was lying unconscious somewhere aft. The interrupter bars of the mid-upper turret had been torn off, so he couldn't safely fire his guns; the aerials had gone, so the wireless operator could neither transmit nor receive.

"bloody great chunks out of the wings"

Those were the bits I knew about: it was later that I learned about the loss of mainplane rivets and various other bits and pieces.

The navigator came through on the intercom. He reckoned we were heading straight for Bremen, and would rather we were not. Slowly, I kicked Baker Two round until she was heading roughly west-south-west, and we staggered on towards the German coast. A night-fighter spotted us, and moved into position to attack. I looked around for a cloud to hide in, but clouds are like policemen – all around when you don't need them, but…

I stood Baker Two on a wing-tip with the rudders and the engines, first one way then the other, and the fighter went away, probably unwilling to tangle with a maniac. Ten minutes later, at three o'clock in the morning, the bomb-aimer said there was an island just ahead. "Goodoh," said the navigator, "that'll be Heligoland. I'll give you a new course in a moment, Jack."

For him, Heligoland was a useful pin-point; for me, and every other pilot in Bomber Command, it was a hot spot, armed with batteries of searchlights and anti-aircraft guns, and some very hostile *Kannonieren*. The searchlight master beam crept towards us, swept the starboard wing, and fastened on. The two slave beams were quick to join the fun. Baker Two was coned, and the flak was sure to follow. Each 88 millimetre shell would produce a thousand white-hot fragments, any one of which could make a hole in a Lancaster – and in us – at a hundred yards range.

With a fully-fit aircraft, we might have stood a chance: in Baker Two's condition, the prospects were not good. I did what I could in the way of evasive action with what strength remained, but the twinkling, lethal bursts came nearer all the time. Then a strange thing happened – so strange that at first I thought it must be an optical illusion. Some 2,000 feet above us, slightly ahead to port and on a parallel course, another Lancaster appeared, flying straight and level, right through the top of the beam that was holding Baker Two. Immediately, as though some Feldwebel down there on the ground had rapped out a command, the slave beams and the anti-aircraft gunners switched their attention to this other prey. Kicking Baker Two back on course for England, and easing her nose down to gain a bit more speed, I watched the shells bursting around that sacrificial Lancaster. The extraordinary thing was that the pilot took no action, that he seemed oblivious to what was going on. Were they all asleep in there? Or were they dead, with the auto-pilot flying the aircraft? Whatever the reason, their arrival on the scene could not have been more timely, nor their presence more propitious; but for them, the odds were that Baker Two would have been blown out of the sky. I could not tear my eyes away as our saviours in that aircraft flew serenely on. The shells were bursting all around her, and I waited to see the flames begin, to see the tanks explode, to see the crew bale out, but nothing like that happened. That Lancaster simply disappeared. One moment she was there, shining in the searchlights, surrounded by the flak; the next moment, she was gone. No fire, no explosion, no trace of parachutes – just the darkness of the night and nothing more.

By then, Baker Two was beyond the range of the *Kannonieren*, and going hard for home. I was still

puzzling about what had happened and how we had survived when we reached the airfield circuit, and made a very shaky landing. I knew I'd seen that Lancaster, and clearly the searchlight and flak crews saw her, too. But where did she come from, and where did she go? The thought came to my mind that she was a ghostly aircraft, flown by a ghostly crew. Perhaps the pilot was a friend from days in training, who had got the chop (and there were several of those around, after the Battle of the Ruhr). I didn't mention these conjectures to the de-briefing officer, nor to the crew. In fact, I haven't mentioned them to anyone up until this time.

As for Baker Two (her registration was DV190), the people from A.V. Roe's were surprised and pleased to see she had survived. They replaced her ailerons, aerials, interrupter bars, flap jacks and rivets, and sent her back to duty just in time for the Battle of Berlin. Manned by another crew, she went down somewhere over Germany on 21st January 1944. That time, perhaps, there was no helpful, ghostly bomber there to intervene.

The next story comes from Ken Goodchild, one-time wireless operator/air gunner (usually abbreviated to Wop/Ag) of No. 51 Squadron, based at Snaith, near Selby in what is now South Yorkshire. He was shot down over Duisburg during the Battle of the Ruhr in May 1943, and spent the next two years and more in a German prisoner-of-war camp. This story, however, which he calls "The Wimpey that was frightened of the sea," concerns an event in 1942, while he and his crew were still under training at Cottesmore OTU.

"Our operational training course consisted of cross-country flights of four or five hours duration, day and night, fighter affiliation, dummy attacks with 25 pound bombs, and some practice attacks to exercise the ground defences in tracking aircraft. On the day in question, we were to carry out a cross-country flight from Cottesmore to Weston-super-Mare on the Bristol Channel, up the Welsh coast, over Snowdonia, on to Glasgow, across to Edinburgh and finally southward back to base. A simple, straight forward exercise, or so we thought.

The Flight Commander said that the Wellington assigned to us had just had a major overhaul, and therefore we were to do a war-load test climb. That meant we had full fuel tanks, and a full bomb-load simulated by bomb cases filled with sand. We were to test fuel consumption, rate of climb, stalling speeds, and all the equipment.

The cockpit layout in the Wimpey was that I, as the wireless operator, sat behind the pilot, and the navigator behind me. I was responsible for monitoring the fuel gauges, which were on the starboard cabin wall, and readings had to be taken every thirty minutes. All went well until we reached the coast near Weston-super-Mare, when I checked the gauges and found we had very little fuel left. We assumed we had a serious leak, and looked for somewhere to put down. Close by was an army co-operation airfield called Weston Zoyland. It was only a small grass field, but it was all we had, and we went in and landed.

It took them three days to refuel us with jerry cans. No leaks were found, and we could not understand what had happened to our fuel. Meanwhile, the people there were sufficiently impressed by having a real bomber on their field

between them, and also to lend us his team of plough horses. They were attached by a rope to the tail-wheel assembly and, with the help of local volunteers, the aircraft was gently eased back into the farmer's field until 200 yards had been added to the take-off run.

We had to start the engines on the internal batteries, which was not recommended owing to their limited capacity. However, all went well, and we were ready to go, aiming at the gap in the hedge. The skipper held the brakes on until the engines were going at full bore. The take-off run was a bit bumpy but the undercarriage held up, and away we went, having overflown the field to wave to our friends below.

Back at Cottesmore, the Flight Commander wanted to know the whole story. When we told him, he said that the aircraft had been on an operational squadron, that it had been badly damaged twice and two members of its crew had been killed. After that, it had kept developing faults whenever it crossed the coast, and nothing seemed to put it right. It would fly all day over land and never give any problem. The engines had been changed and the fuel system overhauled, and it was sent to Cottesmore. That was when we had been given the job of testing it.

After what happened, it was decided that the aircraft would not be flown again, and it was cannibalised for spares. It seems impossible that a piece of machinery could have feelings, but it was as though this aircraft had been hurt enough, and was afraid to cross water in case it got hurt again."

to treat us to a slap-up lunch in Weston town hall on the Sunday. We hadn't the heart to tell them we were only under training, and carrying sand-filled bombs.

When we had been re-fuelled, and ready to go back to base, another problem reared its head. We had to take-off from the field without damaging the aircraft. Fortunately, the farmer who owned the adjacent field agreed to cut down the hedge

Jack Knott, another Wop/Ag, was one of Ken Goodchild's companions through gunnery training at Pembrey in South Wales and at Cottesmore. At Pembrey, flying in short-nosed Bristol Blenheims, they fired off hundreds of rounds at towed drogue targets from their two-gun turrets. Stoppages were always likely to occur, and Knott had more than his fair share. Indeed, he had so many that he was known to one and all as "One-shot Knott". Nor did his misfortunes end at gunnery school, as Ken Goodchild describes.

"The Wop's job on take-off in a Wimpey was to keep an eye on the flare-chute until the plane was airborne, because the flares had a nasty habit of slipping out. On one occasion, Jack was standing by the flare-chute while the pilot ran the engines prior to take-off, holding position on the brakes. When the pilot let the brakes go and the Wimpey shot forward, Jack slipped, and fell through the push-out escape hatch in the fuselage wall. When the aircraft was airborne, the pilot made a routine intercom check, and found that he was short of a wireless op.

Fortunately, Jack wasn't hurt, and he went on to a Wimpey squadron while I went through 1663 HCU and eventually on to No.51 Squadron. We didn't meet again until the European war was over, and we were both at a rehabilitation unit. Then he told me the story of his Wimpey tour, and in particular about one trip to the "Happy Valley", when they had been badly damaged and were making for the Kent coast. All through the trip, the crew had been complaining about someone fooling about. Jack said it was worrying, as though someone or something was standing behind them, and watching them.

Near the Kent coast they called "Mayday", and were told to fly over the coast, turn the aircraft back to sea and bale out. A Spitfire from Manston would come up and shoot the Wimpey down once they were out. They all jumped successfully, and the Spit went in to knock the Wimpey down, but when it approached from the rear, the Wimpey's tail guns returned the fire. The Spit pilot must have been surprised, but he tried again with a head-on attack, and was met by fire from the front turret. At last the Spit dived in from above, and managed to set fire to the Wimpey, which at last went down into the Channel.

I reckon some ghostly gunner was showing Jack how to fire more than one shot."

The next story comes from David Bannister's file, and it is set in western Germany, at RAF Bruggen where, in the late 1960s, the English Electric twin-jet Canberras of No. 213 Squadron were being replaced by American-built Phantoms. The last two Canberras were standing on their dispersals, ready to be flown back to England, one by Wing Commander Mike Chandler with his navigator, and the second by another crew. On the evening before the flight was due, an RAF policeman telephoned Chandler in the officers' mess to report that the door of one of the aircraft was open. Chandler had checked both aircraft earlier, and had been sure that the doors were secure; nevertheless, he drove to the dispersal, where he was met by a Police Corporal complete with dog. Together, they inspected the Canberras, and tried the doors: both were securely locked.

The Wing Commander, naturally, wished to

know why he had been called out of the mess when there was clearly nothing wrong. The Corporal explained that he had at first been alerted by the behaviour of his dog which, while he was patrolling the dispersal, had pricked up its hackles and begun to bark. "It was when I led the dog between the first two aircraft," said the Corporal, "that I noticed the door of the one behind was open."

When Chandler pointed out that there were only two Canberras on the dispersal, indeed on the airfield, the Corporal insisted that a third had been standing there when he started his patrol. Admittedly, it was not there now, and he had neither seen nor heard it leave. Then, the Corporal's face brightened. "I made a note of its serial number," he said, and pulled a notebook from his pocket. "Look, sir, there it is." Chandler read the number: it was not that of either of the aircraft remaining on the dispersal.

Next day, the last two Canberras were flown away as scheduled. Strangely, the screen of the watching ground radar showed three aircraft flying together, although neither Chandler nor the other airmen saw another aircraft near them on their flight. Later, the number noted by the Corporal was traced: it was that of a 213 Squadron

A 213 squadron Canberra

Canberra which had crashed at the end of the runway at Bruggen some years earlier. The pilot and the navigator had both died in the crash.

The three American-built fighter aircraft employed in combat over Europe by the United States Army Air Force during World War II were the Lockheed P-38 Lightning, the Republic P-47 Thunderbolt and the North American P-51 Mustang. Each of these aircraft had different characteristics, different performances and very different appearances. The Thunderbolt, with its big Pratt & Whitney radial engine and bulky fuselage (which brought it the name of "The Jug"), had a comparatively slow rate of climb, and did not have the range to escort the bombers much further than the Ruhr, but it was a formidable adversary in combat; the Mustang, powered by a Packard Merlin liquid-cooled engine, was the sleekest and the fastest of the three, and proved to be the best long-range escort fighter of its day. The Lightning, powered by two liquid-cooled Allisons, with the pilot housed in a nacelle between twin booms, was the first to arrive in the European theatre, and although the USAAF's Fighter Group pilots flew it with bravery and skill, it was never quite fast or manoeuvrable enough to match the

Me-109s or FW-190s. It is, however, the remarkable performance of a Lockheed Lightning, as described by Martin Caidin in "The Fork-Tailed Devil: The P-38", which provides the final story in this chapter.

A patrolling flight of Lightnings, based in North Africa, were engaged in combat by German fighters over the Mediterranean. When the dog-fight ended, and the flight reformed, one Lightning was missing. None of the pilots had seen it go down, and a search of the area revealed no sign of a survivor. Back at base, the loss was recorded and, after it was judged that the pilot's fuel would be exhausted, he was posted "MIA" – missing in action. Then, the air-raid alarm sounded, and the ground radar station picked up a single aircraft approaching the field, low and fast. The anti-aircraft guns were manned, but while the pilots on readiness were still running to their aircraft, the intruder came in sight. It was the missing Lightning, flying in a shallow dive, with its engines at full throttle.

Above the middle of the field, the Lightning seemed to stagger in the air. There was no explosion and no fire, but the aircraft simply broke apart. The watching air, ground and crash crews raised a cheer as a body fell away and a parachute canopy billowed out above it,

but the cheering stopped when it was seen that the figure hung limply in the harness as it drifted down to collapse beside the wreckage.

The pilot had a bullet-hole in the centre of his forehead, and the Medical Officer said he had been dead for several hours. The Engineering Officer found that the tanks of the Lightning were bone-dry, and had been for some time.

All those on the airfield, including over a hundred officers and enlisted men, had witnessed the incident, knew it to be impossible for a dead pilot to fly his aircraft back to base, with no fuel in the tanks, then to pull the rip-cord of his parachute. Nevertheless, they saw it happen, and they later signed their names to that effect on the Base Commander's report of the event.

A Maurice Farman Longhorn

The Montrose Ghost and Others

The story of the Montrose ghost is older than the RAF itself. It first gained currency in 1916, when the junior service was still the Royal Flying Corps. The flying school at Montrose lay on the east coast of Scotland, in a bleak, windswept landscape by the mouth of the river South Esk, some thirty miles north-east of Dundee. There have been differing versions of the story, but as it was originally told, and passed down through the years from one generation of airmen to the next, it concerned a young pupil who showed signs of apprehension about taking that first great step in the making of a pilot – solo flight. His instructor, however, was satisfied with the boy's performance in the Maurice Farman trainers, and pronounced him ready to take the sky alone. The pupil still demurred, but the instructor insisted – the way instructors do – and a first solo flight was duly authorised.

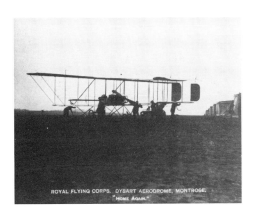

ROYAL FLYING CORPS. DYSART AERODROME, MONTROSE. "HOME AGAIN."

The biplane took off, and climbed quite safely to three hundred feet. There, the pilot appeared to attempt a turn, but his airspeed was too low. A wing tipped over, the aeroplane fell, and failed to recover from the stall. When they pulled him from the wreckage, the boy was dead. The instructor was horrified, but such things happened in flying training, and they always would. The Flying Corps needed pilots on the Western Front, and Montrose must provide them.

That night, the instructor awoke with the feeling that he was not alone. He sat up in his bed. The boy's figure, in a blood-stained leather flying coat, was standing beside him, gazing at him, not with accusation, nor recrimination, but with a sort of sadness. The instructor screamed, and the figure seemed to drift out of the room.

In the morning, the instructor requested the Commanding Officer for a posting to another unit, and the request was granted. The bedroom was allocated to another officer, whose stay was terminated three nights later when the mute, blood stained figure reappeared. When yet a third occupant was similarly visited, the room was locked and never used again.

"A wing tipped over, the aeroplane fell…"

A Sopwith Camel

Another version of the story (of which there are several) is that the spectral figure is that of one Lieutenant Desmond Arthur, who, when his Be2 crashed at Montrose on 27th May 1913, survived long enough to protest that his aircraft had been sabotaged. The official view, however, and one which was voiced by a Member of Parliament, was that the Lieutenant had been indulging in some unauthorised aerobatics. Nevertheless, he was given a full service funeral in the nearby town, which was attended by all the station personnel. Thereafter, Arthur's ghost continually appeared to confront his former colleagues, and to plead with them to clear his name. When a subsequent enquiry attributed the cause of the accident to faulty maintenance, the vindicated spirit did not reappear. The unhappy student pilot's spectre, however, continued reappearing well into the days of World War II and after. RAF Montrose was remarkable in that it was the only Service station at which new arrivals were officially notified that they might expect to meet a ghost.

Lieutenant Desmond Arthur

A Be2 at Montrose

Lieutenant David Simpkins of the Royal Flying Corps was a level-headed officer, conscientious, and popular with the other pilots of his unit, which, in 1916, was based at Scampton, on the old Roman road known as Ermine Street a few miles north of Lincoln. The unit was equipped with Sopwith Camels, perhaps the most effective, and the best-remembered, British single-engined fighters of the first World War. Simpkins was normally the most equable of men, but his temper had recently been tried by the ceaseless chatter in the mess about one or the other of the Montrose ghosts. One afternoon in August, when the subject turned yet again to the death and reappearance of Lieutenant Desmond Arthur, he had stalked out of the ante-room and slammed the door behind him.

That sort of behaviour, unusual in Simpkins, was the normal pattern for his colleague, Lieutenant Peter Salter. It was not that Salter was in any way ill-tempered, in fact he was good-natured to a fault; he was just a very noisy officer. Under Salter's touch, door-knobs always rattled

Montrose, 1915

Scampton, 1996

Scampton, November 1917

and doors banged shut or open; under his footsteps, stairways always groaned and creaked. Although not overweight, he was seemingly incapable of quiet or silent movement.

It was on 7th December, some four months after Simpkins's little show of temper, that Salter left the flight office, saying that he proposed to take an aircraft on the practice firing range. Simpkins settled by the stove with a book, hoping to enjoy a peaceful morning. Within half-an-hour, however, both the silence and his hopes were shattered, when Salter flung the door open: "I'm not going on the range," he said. "I've got to take an aircraft to Tadcaster. I'll be back in time for tea. Cheerio!"

No sooner had he slammed the door behind him than he was banging on the window, and shouting for his maps, which lay on the office table. Simpkins passed them through the window, and settled down again. The morning passed and, after lunch in the mess, Simpkins returned to the office and his book. It was at 3.45 p.m. that an unusual thing occurred: the door opened silently, and Salter stood in the threshold, in his flying kit. "Hello," he said.

"Hello," said Simpkins. "That didn't take you long. Good trip?" Salter nodded and, with the usual "Cheerio", left as silently as he had come. Simpkins was amazed. Could it be that all the comments and complaints about his mess-mate's elephantine behaviour were finally having some effect?

Some fifteen minutes later, another officer, Lieutenant Garner-Smith, came into the office. "I hope Peter gets back soon," he said. "We're going into Lincoln this evening."

"He is back," said Simpkins. "He may be in the locker-room, or having tea."

That evening, Simpkins travelled into Lincoln on his own, and entered the lounge of the Albion Hotel. A group of Scampton officers were talking at a table, and Simpkins heard the words "Crash" and "Tadcaster". Quickly, he joined them. "Excuse me, chaps," he said, "couldn't help overhearing. Has there been a crash?"

"Afraid so," one of the group replied. "The word came through just before we left the station. Peter Salter's dead – crashed on the way to Tadcaster. They found him in the wreckage. Apparently his wrist watch was smashed, and it had stopped at twenty-five past three."

Twenty-seven years later, Scampton was the base from which the hand-picked crews of No. 617 Squadron flew to attack the Ruhr dams with Barnes Wallis's bouncing bomb; later, in peace-time, Scampton housed the Central Flying School and the Red Arrows formation aerobatic team. When I visited it then, to make a TV documentary about its splendid history, Scampton was a busy, thriving station. Now, it seems that the RAF has no further use for it, and as to what will happen to the famous airfield and the hangars, to the mess-halls and control tower, no-one knows.

The next short episode relates back to the active years, and it is typical of many which emanate from Scampton.

It was a cold, clear winter's night, and a full

moon was glinting on the airfield through scattered clouds when the Orderly Officer and the Orderly Sergeant were making their tour of inspection. Approaching the control tower, they briefly separated – the officer to look around the front of the building, while the sergeant walked around the back.

As the officer reached the mid-point of his circuit, beneath the high windows which gave the flying control staff their view of the airfield, he was suddenly confronted by a figure, fully dressed in wartime flying kit, with an orange-coloured Mae West and a harness for a chest-type parachute, and carrying a bulky canvas map bag.

The officer halted as the figure walked towards him and, although it seemed so real and solid, he knew at once that he was looking at a ghost. Involuntarily, he shouted, but in the time it took the sergeant to reach him, the figure had vanished from his sight. It was not the sort of incident which lent itself to entry in his report, and he did not record it. Nevertheless, he was satisfied that he had encountered a bomber navigator, who had at last returned to base.

Ground crew of 460 Squadron working on their Lancasters at Binbrook, 1943

Less than twenty miles from Scampton, on the Lincolnshire Wolds south-west of Grimsby, lies what remains of the wartime bomber base of Binbrook, one of only three of No.1 Group's bases that were built to peace-time standards (the others were Elsham Wolds and the Lancaster Finishing School at Hemswell). For most of World War II, Binbrook was the home of No.460 Squadron of the Royal Australian Air Force, and their Lancasters. Nearly five years after VE-Day, when Binbrook was still an active RAF airfield, Trevor Deane of Weston-super-Mare was posted there as an airframe fitter.

This is the story that he told: "At that time, the six hangars were occupied by four squadrons of Lincoln bombers (the Lancaster's successors), Nos.9,12,101 and 617, with second line servicing, plus the Bomber Command Modifications Unit. While on guard duty, several of us were given keys to the squadron hangars and told to check that all the telephones were on their rests, which we did. On returning to the guardroom we found that this was a regular occurrence, and recorded in the incidents log, and that 'anonymous calls' to the guardroom had been going on for years. The 'calls' only came at night, and there was never a voice at the other end.

On windy nights, the hangar doors could be heard rattling at the transmitting end, indicating that the telephone hand-set was off the rest, yet the guards sent to investigate never found this to be so.

The service police were quite accustomed to

Binbrook, 1996

these incidents, and informed us that the calls were made by 'Clubfoot', supposed to be an Australian armourer NCO during the war, who had been injured by the carelessness of a pilot, and had sought revenge by attaching an explosive device to the pilot's Lancaster bomb-load, but had blown himself up in the process.

'Clubfoot' was also frequently seen limping along the perimeter track, sometimes attempting to flag down vehicles (whose drivers invariably accelerated away).

Many duty armourers, on a sleeping-in overnight duty at the bomb dump, testified to being woken by the incessant ringing of the gate bell, and by the rattling of the chained and padlocked gates, only to find no human presence when they reached the gates."

I could recount a hundred stories of that sort. Different localities, different times, different personnel, but with a similar basic scenario: The inexplicable sounds of movement or of voices, the gates or doors that shut and open by themselves, the trained guard dogs that will not enter certain buildings; then there are the spectral visitations, often accompanied by a sudden drop in temperature, the recognition by the witness of flying clothes or equipment, and the subsequent disappearance. The realist in me is obliged to ask – does one tale spawn another, then another and another? Could it be that, if an old airfield does not yield a ghost, one must be invented for it? "My old base has a headless sergeant, who rides around the perimeter track on a motor-bike." "Really? There are two officers of mine who fight a pistol

duel on the old parade ground, while the WAAF they are fighting over stands by, weeping." No, that is a momentary lapse into levity, possibly forgivable at this point in the story, but unworthy of the subject. The fact is that neither of the airfields from which I flew on operations, Wickenby and Wyton, seem to have had a ghost of any kind – not that I know of, anyway. Further, the tales I have quoted, and will quote later, have been authenticated by serious men, not given to imaginings, and certainly not to fabrication.

In 1949, C. Stephenson-Mole was the driver of a "Queen Mary" heavy transport vehicle, engaged in crash recovery and based at Rufforth, a few miles west of York. "The MT section," he wrote, "was in a building on the road to Askham where there was also a hangar for storing the vehicles. One evening that summer, I had parked in the hangar and was leaving through the side door, midway down the length of the hangar, when I was pushed in the rear by another driver rushing out. When I asked why he was in such a hurry, he said he'd had a 'funny' experience, and I noticed that he seemed panic-stricken and his face was white. He said he had followed me into the hangar, left his vehicle parked along the side, and stopped at the side-door to take out his cigarettes. He found that he didn't have a light. He heard talking and, looking around, saw a group of six or seven persons laughing and chatting and smoking in the corner of the hangar. They were in flying gear, which he thought was strange, but then he remembered that crane operators sometimes wore old aircrew Sidcot suits for protective clothing. He

Stan Smith BEM, who tried to rescue the Hildreth family from the "Grasslands" farmhouse

walked up to them, only to find that they seemed to melt away. At that, he panicked and ran back to the exit. I went back into the hangar, and confirmed that there was no-one there. I was subsequently told that during the war a bomber had crashed on a farmhouse some fifty yards or so beyond the hangar." When that tragic accident occurred, Rufforth was an operational training unit, dedicated to the task of enabling embryo bomber crews to make the transition from twin-engined aircraft to the four-engined Halifaxes with which No. 4 Group's squadrons, based on eleven airfields to the east and south of York, were currently equipped. On 16th November 1944, a rolling mist across the airfield was making landings difficult for experienced pilots, let alone for those who were in the learning process.

When Halifax JP128 struck "Grasslands", as the farmhouse was called, three of the occupants were killed, and the young son of the family, scrambling down a drainpipe from his bedroom, was the sole survivor. The aircraft, meanwhile, ploughed on across the airfield like a juggernaut, destroying two more bombers and a fire truck on its way, and six of the seven-man crew were killed.

Rufforth airfield is now the home of a busy gliding school, a fleet of private aircraft and a swarm of microlights. When I called there last April to beg a flight around the area, Richard Boddy, the chairman of the flying club, produced the visitor's book for signature. Then followed two of the strange coincidences which have kept cropping up in the writing of these stories. First, the "Remarks" column against the last five entries in the book read: "We were the next crew to land

"Grasslands", still showing the scars where the Halifax struck

The path of the Halifax across Rufforth

after the aircraft that hit the farmhouse." That was no more than happen stance, but the next was sad: Dick Boddy told me that the surviving son of the "Grasslands" family had died a week ago, killed in a road accident while travelling to the funeral of a friend.

Talking subsequently with members, I learned that, a few years earlier, a dozen of them had gathered in the hangar and made use of a Ouija board. They had received a message from the son of the "Grasslands" family who had died in 1944. "I shall be standing on the runway," he had imparted, "at midnight on the next summer solstice." They were there, but he was not. It was only later, and too late, that somebody remembered the difference between British Summer Time in the 1990s and the Double British Summer Time of fifty years ago.

Rufforth main runway, 1996

Airmen at Bircham Newton, 1933.
Behind a Fairey Gordon of 207 Squadron

Here is one more story before this chapter closes, and it comes from the pages of The Eastern Daily Press of 12th March 1986. It seems that the old RAF base at Bircham Newton, lying on the Norfolk coast south of the Wash, and dating from the days of World War I, boasted two squash courts, as did many stations of that era, one of which had been haunted for over forty years. Following reports of strange sounds being heard, the BBC sent a crew to set up a microphone. The sound-man, while waiting, stepped down into the court to hit a ball about himself. The temperature fell suddenly, and "he spun round to see an airman in full wartime flying gear watching him from the viewing gallery". A team of investigators installed a recording apparatus, and this picked up noises which were not to be expected in a deserted place. "They picked up footsteps coming down the stairs, but...it would have been necessary to open a door to reach the stairs, and the door was closed". The next sounds recorded were of a bomber pilot talking to control, with the drone of aero-engines in the background. The investigators found that the hauntings had begun in World War II, and that three airmen, all keen squash players, had been killed when their bomber crashed near Bircham Newton church. "I think what they are doing," said a member of the team, "is trying to attract attention, because they need our help." That is one interpretation of the haunting; I prefer this alternative explanation: the airmen, enjoying an evening in the mess, and not entirely sober, had drawn up an agreement that, if they should die, they would always get together at their favourite venue on the base.

A final comment came from a spokesman for the Construction Industry Training Board, who then owned the station. This solid citizen was reported to have said: "We are well-used to the ghosts, but I don't wish to comment further."

The First Class cabin of an L-1011 Tristar

Flight 401

There is no good time to crash an aeroplane, nor is there a good place, but if you had to choose the worst of times and places, the middle of the night and a wilderness of swampland would probably come high up on the list. To do that, however, was the fate of Captain Bob Loft of Eastern Airlines when, on the approach path to Miami International Airport, a few miles to the east, he crashed the Lockheed L-1011 Tristar jetliner No. 310 in the middle of the swamp on the southern tip of Florida known as the Everglades.

The story of Tristar 310, which left Kennedy Airport in New York as EAL Flight 401 at 9.20 p.m. on Friday 29th December 1972, gives instances, more recent but not totally dissimilar to those of the R101's first major flight not only of forebodings of disaster, but of later visitations from, and communication with, the "other side".

Captain Loft was in his mid-fifties, and, with nearly 30,000 flying hours in his logbook, was one of the most experienced and senior of Eastern Airlines' pilots. With him in the Tristar's lofty cockpit were his 1st and 2nd Officers, Bert Stockstill and Don Repo, both highly experienced on type, and both sharing his enthusiasm for, and confidence in, the "Whisperliner", as they called the Tristar. Ten stewardesses made up the cabin crew and, of these, two seem to have had some warning of disaster. One had told her colleagues that, in a vivid premonition, she had seen a Tristar crashing in the Everglades while going in to land just before the next New Year; another had been told by a medium that she would be involved in a flying accident, and that she would survive it.

At JFK, there were some last minute cancellations for Flight 401, and the 163 passengers who came aboard that evening by no means filled the Tristar to capacity. After being welcomed aboard by the smartly-dressed, smiling stewardesses, the passengers were shown how to use the emergency equipment and where to find the escape doors. The estimated time of arrival at Miami International, a thousand miles to the south, was 11.32 p.m. and, after a trouble-free flight, the Tristar joined the Miami traffic pattern on schedule for landing. With the gear selected down, Captain Loft turned on final and changed the radio frequency from "Approach" to "Tower". The crew checked the systems, and there was a problem: no green light on the panel from the nose wheel locks. They retracted the gear and tried again: still no green light, and the warning horn confirmed that the nose gear was not locked in the down position. As yet, no-one suspected it, neither in the aircraft nor in Miami Tower, but from that moment onwards, Flight 401 was doomed.

On the radio, Captain Loft reported the malfunction, and told the controller that he was going around again to sort it out. All the time, the aircraft was being flown by the automatic pilot, which could be disengaged at any time by either of the pilots, but which would disengage itself if sufficient pressure were exerted on either of the pilots' manual controls. It made no difference whether the pressure were intended or accidental; it could be caused, for example, by the Captain leaning over to check the little light bulb on the right side of the panel – the light which should be showing green. That, it seems, was exactly what happened. Neither Loft nor Stockstill, nor the auto-pilot, was flying the Tristar as it headed west across the Everglades, and gently started to descend, while the auto-pilot instruments, also disengaged, continued to indicate an altitude of 2,000 feet.

1st Officer Stockstill, meanwhile, was trying unsuccessfully to replace the panel light bulb, and Loft, losing patience, directed 2nd Officer Repo to go below and check the nose gear visually. Angelo Donadeo, an Eastern Airlines technician, who was on board as a passenger and sitting on the "jump-seat" behind Loft, accompanied Repo to give what help he could. Their inspection was inconclusive and, down in the wheel-well, they failed to hear the quiet chime of the bell on Repo's cockpit panel which gave warning of a drop in altitude. In the cockpit, Loft and Stockstill, now overdue for landing, convinced themselves that they had a faulty light bulb, and Loft told Miami that he was coming in. In Miami tower, a quick look at the radar showed

In the cockpit of a Tristar, the landing gear lever, with its three lights underneath, is to the left of the circular radar screen

the ground controller that the Tristar was below 1,000 feet, but he had another six airliners in the traffic pattern, and could not spare the time to make another scan.

Little grows in the Everglades apart from myrtle and willow among the clumps of sawgrass, and little lives there but watersnakes, alligators, and millions of mosquitoes – and frogs. It was for the latter (their legs are regarded as a delicacy by gourmets) that a retired wildlife officer in a flat-bottomed air-boat was hunting, when Flight 401 roared overhead and smashed into the swampland with a blinding flash of light that seemed to last for ever. The time was just after 11.42 p.m. One stewardess's premonition had been right as to the place, and almost as to the time.

Two other pilots in the Miami pattern reported the explosion to approach control, and the nearby Coast Guard helicopter station was immediately alerted. In the Everglades, the frog-hunter, driving his air-boat at top speed, was the first to reach the scene, and it was a glimpse of the faint light from his headlamp that told the leading helicopter pilot where he had to be. He could not, however, set the chopper down: for one thing, his wheels would have sunk into the swamp and, for another, as he

hovered, his rotor roused a hail of metal fragments from the Tristar and showered them around. He stayed in the hover and dropped a paramedic and an airframe mechanic to do the best they could. The other three rescue crews were instructed to set down on the nearest levee, a strip of raised roadway which ran across the swamp some six miles away, and proceed from there.

The scene that met the rescue men was one of total carnage, of a waking nightmare. Bodies lay in heaps among the tangled, knife-sharp wreckage, the dying among the dead, many soaked in jet fuel, some near to drowning in the stagnant, inky water of the swamp, some stripped of clothing by the blast of the explosion. The sounds of suffering – screams and moans and cries for help – came from everywhere. Somewhere in the darkness of the swamp, 176 people were either dead, dying, injured or in deadly danger, and to meet the emergency were one frog-hunter, one airframe mechanic and one paramedic.

The mechanic found the nose section some distance from the body of the aircraft, and made his way inside. The seats had been dislodged by the impact. Stockstill was dead and Captain Loft was lying on the cockpit floor. Although his injuries were not of a mortal kind, he was deep in shock. He told the mechanic that he was going to die and, some minutes later, he did exactly that. Down in the wheel well, Donadeo was conscious, but Repo's skull was fractured, and he was clearly at death's door.

Back in the control tower at Miami International, the full weight of the emergency services was being called into action: Army, Navy,

Air Force, Fire and Ambulance, Police and Public Health, from all parts of Jackson County and the State of Florida. Now, the helicopters could get closer to the scene, because the metal fragments had been sucked down into the swamp and were no longer flying about, and more air-boats were arriving all the time. The rescue team's guide-lines were to ignore the dead, to search for the injured and get them away as fast as possible.

With the first light of morning, the whole scene lay before them. The crumpled wreckage stretched for nearly half a mile, and the landing gear had scoured three long channels through the swamp. The grim work began of finding the bodies, tagging and bagging them, and despatching them to the Jackson County morgue. When all the statistics were to hand, it was found that, of the 176 souls aboard Tristar 310, 99 had died, 60 were in a serious condition, and 17 had minor injuries or none. In due course, the cockpit "black box" was recovered, parts were re-assembled, and survivors recounted what they could remember of the flight's last moments. The investigation showed that the nose gear had never been other than solidly locked down, while questions still remained as to the awkward fitting of the lamp-bulb on the panel, the too quiet altitude warning chime, and the possible accidental disengagement of the automatic pilot.

It was at this point that the writer John G. Fuller began to take an interest in the Tristar tragedy, and to research it with the same thoroughness he would show in studying the mystery of R101. In conversation with Eastern Airlines cabin crews, he discovered that, in the months following the crash, many of the stewardesses had seen Don Repo's face, and sometimes his figure, emanating out of a sort of cloud, close beside them in the aircraft's lower galley. Pursuing the investigation, he found that Repo was also appearing in the cockpit, and always trying to help – suggesting that an electric circuit, or a certain engine, should be checked, and warning of a fault in the hydraulic system. Furthermore, his warnings were consistently well-founded. Once, knocking was heard from the wheel-well, and no-one was surprised when Repo's figure was seen to be down there, and when an engineer, engaged on a minor piece of maintenance, had a tool placed in his hand, he knew well enough that Repo was beside him.

The wreckage of flight 401 scattered across the Everglades.

One of the airline captains heard Repo's voice distinctly, saying "There will never be another L-1011 crash – we won't let it happen." Repo was right – there has been no other serious accident to date. At least four captains recognised Bob Loft – who quickly disappeared – seated with the first-class passengers, and once his voice was heard throughout the aircraft, welcoming the passengers aboard. The strange visitations seemed to be confined to Eastern Airlines Tristars, and occasionally to those lent by EAL to Pan American. No-one, however, was prepared to report the ghostly sights and sounds officially, in case he or she was thought to be mentally unbalanced; such suspicions could lead, at best, to a session with the company psychiatrist and a rest-cure in the "funny farm", or, at worst, to dismissal. However much they felt they had to talk to someone, most of the witnesses were afraid to do so, even to Fuller, despite his promise of confidentiality.

The number of visitations peaked in the June of 1973, then they became less frequent and, by the spring of 1974, they had ceased altogether.

Meanwhile, Fuller had found two Eastern Airlines pilots who were deeply interested in the paranormal, and were New York members of a nation-wide group known as the Spiritual Frontier. Together they attended a seance with a female trance-medium, for what they described as a "soul rescue" exercise, and communication was established with Repo on "the other side". Through the medium, they relived the final moments of Flight 401 with him, ending with the rush of water and the buckling of the nose gear. The medium, at that time, was clearly in distress, and suffering the head pains that Repo must have felt. Nevertheless, the pilots persisted in persuading Repo that he was a spirit, that he must stop trying to stay with the Tristar, and let himself be helped into the after-life, where there were those who wanted to help him. According to the medium, he seemed to be reluctant: he loved his wife and family, and felt bound to them and to the Tristar. Some sessions later, however, he seemed more resigned to the way things had to be, and his last words to the group were of thanks for what they had done.

The spirit of Don Repo, however, was not yet laid to rest. In mid-June 1974, two stewardesses, on a flight in Tristar 318 from Miami to Newark, saw Repo clearly in the galley. As they watched, he stood there for a while, totally impassive, and then disappeared. Tristar 318, as it happened, contained some non-structural bits and pieces – avionics, electrical and, significantly, galley equipment – all of which had been salvaged from the wreck of 310.

The girls were badly shaken, and eventually told their story to a sympathetic listener, Dick Manning, an Eastern Airlines flight engineer, who, in addition to being a practising Christian, was a student of the paranormal scene. Manning decided to go back to basics and try a primeval method of allaying a ghost. He entered the galley of Tristar 318 with a cup of water, sprinkled it around, and called on Repo to appear. That Repo slowly did, out of a cloud, as he had often done before, and Manning told him that he need no longer be there, that he must let himself be guided to where he belonged. At that, Repo's figure was bathed in light and disappeared. Neither his apparition, nor that of Captain Loft, was ever seen again.

Fuller, however, was not entirely satisfied. He and his researcher, after due instruction, resorted to the Ouija board, and called up Repo's spirit. By the answers he gave to their questions on matters of which only he could know, they were utterly convinced that it was really Repo who was talking to them from wherever he might be. Above all, he wanted them to meet his wife and daughter, to tell them that he loved them, and was watching over them.

With some trepidation, Fuller did just that. He arranged a meeting in Miami, where Repo's family lived, and took the Ouija board along. The passages that followed between Repo, his wife Alice and his daughter Donna, while Fuller watched and listened, were full of love and humour, and made a strangely happy ending to the story of Flight 401.

Eastern Airlines Tristar N318EA.
Pieces of avionics, electrical and galley equipment,
salvaged from the wreck of 310, were used in this aircraft

The Watch Tower

The airfield at East Kirkby, which lies inland from Skegness just to the south of the Lincolnshire Wolds, was the wartime home of two No.5 Group squadrons – Nos.57 and 630. The squadrons flew Lancasters, and when the pilots spoke to flying control on the RT they used the airfield call-sign "Silksheen".

In 1958, most of the base reverted to the farmland it had been before the war. Down came the hangars, the workshops and the Nissen huts, away went much of the concrete of the taxiways and of the dispersal pans where the bombers used to stand. But Fred and Harold Panton, whose father had farmed the land pre-war, made it their business to retain the watch-tower, and to return it to its wartime state. It so happened that their elder brother Christopher, a flight engineer, had been killed in the costly attack on Nuremberg on the night of 30th March 1944. It would have been the last operation of his tour; and with many more young victims of the bomber war, he lies in the great, monumentally beautiful Allied war cemetery at Durnbach in Bavaria. The East Kirkby watch tower was to be the Pantons' memorial

Fred and Harold Panton,
and the East Kirkby Watch Tower

to Chris and all who flew and died as he did.

As the years passed, the environs of the watch tower were found to be frequented by the figure of a tall man, wearing a service peaked cap and a USAAF-style leather jacket. When Fred Panton first saw him, late on a summer evening, the figure appeared to be carrying an untidy bundle of paper carrier-bags. "I was a bit puzzled," said Fred, "but I was late for my supper, and he wasn't doing any harm. Later I realised I'd seen the man they talked about." Denis Brown (they call him Den in East Kirkby) was doing a job of soldering on the first floor of the watch tower, in what had been the signals office in the 1940s, when he heard the ground floor entrance door swing open, and footsteps on the stairs, as though someone were ascending to the control room on the first floor. His initial thought was that it must be his work-mate, and he called out: "Is that you, Ron?" There was no answer, the footsteps continued up the stairs, and he heard the control room door open. When Den followed, with the intention of challenging the intruder, he found the room deserted. He knew there was no other

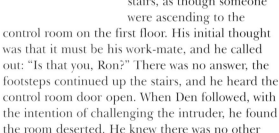

B-17 42-97479 "Belle of Liberty"
at Podington

entrance or exit than through the door at which he stood. A sudden chill struck him, and he made a rapid exit down the stairs and out into daylight. The soldering, he decided, could wait until another day.

There have been many other sightings, one by a group of visitors who had come to admire the Panton brothers' further developments on the old airfield site. They were surprised to see the same strange figure, standing quietly on the watch tower balcony and looking down at them.

The belief has arisen that the visitor is a member of a B-17 Flying Fortress crew who crashed near the airfield on December 30th 1944. Early that morning, thirty-two aircraft of the 92nd Bomb Group, United States Army Air Force, took off from Podington in Bedfordshire to join an attack on a rail bridge at Bulay in western Germany. After forming up and setting course with the 1st Air Division, aircraft 42-97479 "Belle of Liberty" had an engine failure. Its mission was aborted, and the load of six 1,000 pound bombs was jettisoned in the waters of the Wash.

When a second engine failed the pilot decided he could not make it back to Podington, and headed for East Kirkby – the nearest field to his position – where the Lancasters were being fuelled and bombed up for that night's planned attack on a German supply route at Houffalize in Belgium.

Twice the pilot tried to make a landing: twice the flying control officer was not content with his approach, twice a red Very cartridge was fired from the balcony, and twice the voice of "Silksheen" ordered him to go around again. On the third attempt, the B-17 ran out of sky. It crashed on a gently-sloping hillside north-west of the airfield, and burst into flames. The fire was all-enveloping, and although the airfield fire crew hurried to the scene, their resources were inadequate to quench it. All ten men of the aircrew were dead, and their bodies were burned and distorted out of human shape. The belief persists, however, that one man's spirit continued to exist, and that it was the spirit – the unrequited spirit – of the pilot. It is he, they say, who climbs the watch tower stairs, carrying the charred remnants of his parachute, enters the control room, and slams the door behind him. Opinion is that he is seeking the controller who sent him round, and round again, when he was trying to land "Belle of Liberty" on that December morning. However that may be, few who know the story are keen to enter the control room on their own, and only one man has done so after dark.

A few years ago, at the entrance to the field, some surviving airmen of East Kirkby's squadrons erected a memorial to their fallen comrades. The stone bears the numbers of the squadrons and their mottoes (57 Squadron's motto is strangely significant: "Corpus non animum muto" – "My body changes, not my spirit") – and a poem composed by W. Scott, a No. 630 Squadron air gunner.

"I lie here still beneath the hill,
Abandoned long to nature's will.
My buildings down, my people gone,
My only sounds the wild bird's song.

My mighty birds will rise no more,
No more I hear the Merlins' roar,
And never now my bosom feels
The pounding of their giant wheels.

From the ageless hill their voices cast
Thunderous echoes of the past,
And still in lonely reverie
Their great dark wings sweep down to me.

Laughter, sorrow, hope and pain,
I shall never know these things again –
Emotions that I came to know
Of strange young men so long ago.

Who knows, as evening shadows meet,
Are they with me still, a phantom fleet?
And do my ghosts still stride unseen
Across my face so wide and green?

And in the future should structures tall
Bury me beyond recall
I shall still remember them
My metal birds and long-dead men

Now weeds grow high, obscure the sky,
Oh, remember me when you pass by,
For beneath this tangled leafy screen,
I was your home, your friend, 'Silksheen'."

In due course, and after many disappointments, the Pantons purchased one of the few surviving Lancasters, and built a hangar for it. They gathered air memorabilia and established a museum; the control room in the watch tower is authentically furnished and equipped. Still, however, the tower and its environs retain their ghostly aura. On the tarmac apron between the watch tower and the hangar, late at night, bright white spots of light are seen to rise and fall, and to dance from side to side. Despite the local view, which Fred Panton shares, that no-one could spend a whole night in the watch tower, a volunteer came forward in 1994. The offer came from the local old folks' home – an unexpected quarter, if not to say unlikely – and the volunteer was one of the residents. Initially, Fred was doubtful of accepting it. Then, he met the volunteer – a big, powerful man with strong features and a completely shaven head. He was also an ex-member of the SAS. Fred still had his doubts: "What about the staff at the home," he asked, "and the nurses? Don't they mind you doing this?". "They put me up to it," the volunteer replied, "and they're going to lock me in." The selected night was Hallowe'en. The volunteer was installed in the control room which covers most of the first floor. A camp bed was provided, and there was access to the wash-room on the ground floor. At the last moment, the volunteer drew Fred aside:

Memorabilia in the East Kirkby museum

"You say these things," he whispered, "on the spur of the moment, and then you wish you hadn't."

The doors were duly locked, and one of the nurses confided in Fred: "I'm sure he's got paler and paler in the last few days." Fred shook his head in some concern, but the assembled nurses marched happily away. Next morning, when the volunteer emerged, he seemed in good order. "You've proved me wrong," said Fred, and shook him by the hand. "Well done. Did you pass a good night?"

"Didn't sleep much. I saw some lights outside, about ten o'clock."

"That would be me," said Fred, "on my rounds in the Land Rover. Was there nothing else?"

"A couple of times I heard sounds, one at midnight and again at five o'clock. It was as though something like a trolley was being wheeled across the floor. And there was a sort of tinkling, like cups and spoons and saucers."

That, I thought, when Fred told me the story earlier this year, would have been the junior WAAF on duty, wheeling in the tea-break for the control room staff, just the way she had done over fifty years ago. "You know the SAS motto, Fred," I said. 'Who dares, wins.' How did he seem that morning?"

"All right, as far as I could tell. Of course, I couldn't see if he'd gone white – not with that shaven head of his."

61

REMEMBERING
ALL WHO SERVED WITH
55 BASE
5 GROUP - BOMBER COMMAND

EAST KIRKBY
57 & 630 Squadrons
SPILSBY
44 & 207 Squadrons
STRUBBY
619 Squadron

*A 56 squadron Hurricane
at North Weald*

A Blenheim of 25 squadron

The Legends of North Weald

In the autumn of 1940, when the Luftwaffe was exerting all its might in an effort to destroy Britain's air defences, the fighter airfields in the south-east – Manston, West Malling, Hornchurch, Rochford and North Weald – were the first to be attacked. North Weald, on the edge of Epping Forest, as the base of No. 56 and No. 151 Squadron's Hurricanes, and as one of No. 11 Group's sector headquarters, was an important target for the Heinkel 111s, Dornier 215s and Junkers 88s that came over in their hundreds. When the first attack fell in August, a number of airmen decided that they might be safer in the forest depths, and began a minor, and highly unofficial, exodus. The voice of the CO, Wing Commander Victor Beamish, was heard on the Tannoy, and everyone recognised his Ulster accent: "Any man who leaves his post is a coward and a rat – and I shoot rats on sight!" It had been a brief aberration, and no man ever left his post thereafter.

The first ghost story in this chapter is set in those days, and is one of those so carefully researched by David Bannister of Warboys.

A badly damaged Hurricane limped back to

North Weald, 1997

North Weald, crashed on landing and burst into flames. The crew of the crash tender managed to drag the pilot clear, but he had been severely injured and had lost a lot of blood. There was nothing the medical officer could do to save his life. He was placed on a stretcher and carried to an outer office in the nearest building.

The pilot was desperately trying to speak, and the MO, with his ear against the dying man's mouth, was just able to gather that he had to telephone somebody in London. At that moment, the MO was called into the inner office and, while he was speaking to an NCO there, the sound of a body crashing to the floor came from the outer office. Hurrying back, the MO was horrified to discover that the pilot had somehow dragged himself to a wall-mounted telephone and had used the last of his strength to pull down the receiver. Then he had collapsed and was dead within seconds, while the receiver hung beside him, swinging on its cord.

The incident was to leave its echoes at North Weald: many times afterwards, people working in that inner office would hear the body falling and go in to find the telephone receiver hanging off the hook.

Some years later, in the early 1970s, North Weald was the setting for some of the scenes in the epic film "The Battle of Britain", in which a troupe of excellent artists appeared, including Laurence Olivier in the role of the then fighter chief, Air Chief Marshal Sir Hugh Dowding. By that time, the RAF had abandoned the airfield, some of the utilities had been cut off and the telephones removed, but most of the station buildings were still in good repair (as I remember from the years when I ran air shows there).

The trouble with airfields is that they stretch for quite a distance, and the film directors found that when they needed an actor, a technician or an extra, that individual was liable to be a mile or more away. Tiring of bellowing through megaphones and waving arms about, the directors decided to install field telephones on site. This ploy, however, was only partially successful for, as often as not, the extension required was found to be engaged. Then, when the exasperated film maker drove to the location, he would find that the receiver had been taken off the instrument.

The few who knew the story could not help but wonder whether, after thirty years, the Hurricane pilot was still trying to make his vital call to London.

The next North Weald story comes from D.G. Williams of Kempsey, Worcester, and it was first published in the RAF News of 17th November 1995. I am grateful to the writer for his permission to reproduce it here.

"In 1940 I'm sure that if anyone had admitted to believing in ghosts he would either have been accused of being 'bomb-happy' or of trying to 'work his ticket'. I myself had never believed in apparitions until an incident occurred in 1975 which made me change my mind. I have never mentioned it to anyone before.

I was a regular airman, having enlisted at the age of 17 about nine months prior to the outbreak of war. I was posted as a flight rigger to No. 25 Squadron, Fighter Command, late in 1939. The Squadron was then at Northolt, and we later moved to North Weald.

We were equipped with the Bristol Blenheim, the short-nosed fighter version, and we operated as a night-fighter squadron amongst other duties. Whilst at Northolt we carried out one of the first attacks on the enemy – a shoot-up of the sea-plane base at Borkum. While we were at North Weald we had a detachment at Martlesham Heath, and aircraft, aircrew and ground crew were rotated every few weeks, but we could swap about between ourselves, so it was possible for those who preferred North Weald, especially the Londoners, to remain there.

We ground crews had plenty of trips in Blenheims, both official and unofficial. We were usually allocated to a particular aircraft, and flew on air tests and on trips to Martlesham Heath to take spares, etc. I have a record of all my flying hours, and the pilot I flew with most was Pilot Officer Hogg. For example, on 20th March 1940, we flew for an hour on what was known as 'AA co-op' – anti-aircraft co-operation. I had a similar trip with him on 1st April, and this time we were up for two hours. On 10th April, I flew with him again on a thirty-minute air test, and this was one of the official flights for which you had the legitimate loan of a parachute. My last flight with

Blenheim I's of 25 squadron seen here at RAF Hornchurch, August 1939

Fighter pilot of 56 squadron scrambling at North Weald

Pilot Officer Hogg was on 8th June when we paid a quick visit to Northolt. Of course, I had other trips with various pilots, but the outstanding thing about Pilot Officer Hogg was that he went out of his way to obtain a parachute for the ground crew when they were just going up for a ride. I was eighteen by this time, and I think he was about twenty.

On 3rd September 1940, three of our Blenheims returning to North Weald on the change-over were mistaken for Junkers 88s, and shot down by Hurricanes. Pilot Officer Hogg was killed. The air gunner with him that day was Sergeant Powell, and he parachuted to safety. The wreckage of the Blenheim L1512 was put in a corner of the Squadron hangar. The ground crew who worked with Pilot Officer Hogg were all upset by his death; he was very popular with us all. What made matters worse was the fact that it was the result of a tragic mistake.

In the summer of 1975, I thought about making a return to North Weald. Why pick North Weald out of all the RAF stations I had served on before going to France? The reason was that the events which took place there were etched into my mind. The several bombing attacks, the land mine which drifted down and failed to explode, the outstanding Station Commander, Victor Beamish, and the thrill of seeing the Hurricanes of Nos. 56 and 151 Squadrons taking off after being 'scrambled'.

I made enquiries about North Weald and discovered it was being used by several firms engaged in business ventures; also a gliding club was using the base. I was advised to write to the landlords of the airfield, who were the Property Services Agency at Peterborough. In due course, I received a permit which allowed me access to the field. I booked in for a couple of nights at a nearby motel, and drove to the field. I showed my permit to the gatekeeper, who said there were dozens of people who called in and asked if they could look round, and I was the first one to come with a permit. I went round to the far side of the airfield, and noted that the air-raid shelters at the rear of the aircraft pens were still there. My mind went back to 1940, and the times we had to take cover in those shelters.

I drove back to the main camp and had a look round. It all looked familiar except for the absence of aircraft. I spent a couple of nostalgic hours, and got back in my car prior to driving out of the camp. As I attempted to close the door, it seemed as though someone was holding on to it; there was no wind about, so that was a bit spooky. I got out of the car, and was aware of a presence; it was a shadowy figure, surrounded by mist, which reminded me of someone.

Suddenly the mist cleared and I saw Pilot Officer Hogg as clear as a bell. He was holding a flying helmet in his hand. Again the mist appeared, Pilot Officer Hogg vanished, and so did the mist. Although it was a bit upsetting, at no time did I feel nervous.

I know the mind plays funny tricks, but I have no doubt it was Pilot Officer Hogg I encountered on that summer day, thirty-five years after his death."

"Early in 1954," writes Gerald Betts (known to his friends as 'Taff') of Bryncoch, near Neath, "I was posted to RAF North Weald, and I was billeted in a two-storey H-type barrack block, which has since been demolished, in the corner of the airfield near North Weald railway station. Two squadrons of the Royal Auxiliary Air Force were based on the airfield, and the regular airmen like me who serviced the aircraft lived in this block, No. 601 Squadron on the top floor, and No. 604 on the ground floor. During World War II, the building had been a WAAF block, and when one of the wings of the block was hit by a bomb, a WAAF was killed. I was told that the body was buried in the cemetery of St. Andrew's church, about three-quarters of a mile away, and there is a grave there with dates that accord with that.

That WAAF's ghost was said to haunt the barrack block, and sometime in either 1955 or 1956 one of the electrical mechanics was walking along the top floor corridor when he heard the clip, clop of female feet walking on the concrete floor behind him. He was so certain of it that he moved to the side of the corridor to let her pass. No-one passed, and when he looked round, there was no-one there.

At each end of the corridor, there were flights of stairs, with a sort of rubberised surface on which footsteps would have been very quiet. He was so sure that he had heard the steps in the corridor that he looked all around the block, checked the store-rooms and went into all the dormitory rooms to ask if a female had just left. No result. He returned to the room that I was in, and recounted his experience. That was when I had to tell him about the WAAF's ghost. That shook him a bit."

Personnel of 601 and 604 squadrons with their Meteor F8s at North Weald

A Bristol Brigand, the torpedo fitted underneath the fuselage,
photographed in 1947

The Bannister Files

The stories in this chapter are a miscellany, with no particular connection and no central theme. They arise from the researches carried out over the years by David Bannister of Warboys. He calls the first "Phantom Footprints", and it is set in the year of 1947. At that time, Britain was still striving to recover from the damage that five years of war had wrought on her economy. Many foodstuffs were still strictly rationed, as were clothing, all sorts of furnishings, and petrol for the private motorist. They were times of austerity, and not a lot of fun. The National Insurance bill had yet to be enacted, and the Health Minister, Aneurin Bevan, was engaged in trying to persuade the BMA that a National Health Service would not ruin their careers, and might even benefit their patients. Overseas, British troops were engaged in the thankless task of keeping peace in Israel, and Lord Louis Mountbatten was still Viceroy of India, although not for very much longer. The traitor William Joyce (Germany's "Lord Haw-Haw") had been hanged in London, while the Nazi warlords were awaiting the outcome of their trial in Nuremberg.

As for the Royal Air Force, it was in a state of flux and, despite the threat from behind the Iron Curtain, it was not the mighty force it had been in 1945. The new jet V-bombers were not yet in production, and most of the bomber squadrons, at less than a third of their wartime strength, were equipped with the Avro Lincoln – a slightly larger and more unwieldy version of the Lancaster.

Such was the Britain which awaited navigator Warrant Officer Alan Fisher when he returned from a tour of duty in the Middle East. He was hoping to be sent on a heavy conversion flying course, but having spent a few days at an aircrew holding unit, he found himself posted to RAF Boscombe Down in Wiltshire as an accounts clerk in the stores. Fisher, and others in the same position, felt a measure of resentment, and some were so humiliated that they tried to hide the badges of their rank.

For Fisher, the only redeeming feature about Boscombe Down was that it housed a busy flying unit. Aircraft that had come into service towards the end of the war and immediately after it, such as the Avro Tudor and the Bristol Brigand, were being test-flown and evaluated for the peacetime RAF. Whenever he could escape from his clerical duties, Fisher made his way to the flight line, and watched the aircraft being put through their paces. The Brigand, for one, was in the air two or three times a day, seven days a week, flown by a civilian test-pilot from the Bristol Aeroplane Company, with a navigator on loan from the RAF, whom Fisher found it difficult not to regard with envy. On weekdays, the pilot was brought in each morning and taken home each evening in a de Havilland Dragon-Rapide from the BAC airfield at Filton. Fisher assumed that the Rapide pilot eschewed flying on the Sabbath, as on those days an RAF staff car brought him in from Bristol and returned him there.

It was on a Sunday that the Brigand crashed in Lyme Bay while engaged on a torpedo-dropping test. The pilot and the navigator were killed. The RAF driver, waiting on the airfield, was thus tragically relieved of his duty to drive the pilot home. That night he went to bed as usual in one of the long wooden huts, which lay to the west of the airfield's boundary fence, and which provided the other ranks' accommodation.

In the course of the night, the driver and the other twenty airmen in the hut were woken by the sound of footfalls. It sounded as though someone with bare, wet feet was moving to and fro between the beds. The footsteps stopped beside the driver's bed, and he felt a strange force being exerted on his body, which raised him into a sitting position. The room had become bitterly cold. Then the force diminished, the "slap, slap" of the footsteps re-commenced, and died away. When, after several minutes, one of the occupants summoned up the courage to put on the lights, it was seen that a line of wet footprints stretched back to the door across the floor.

The driver reported the incident next morning, and was supported by his room-mates, but his statement was ignored and, when Fisher heard about it in the Sergeants' Mess, it was being regarded with derision by his fellow-NCOs. However, when the hut was haunted by the same sounds and footprints on the next two nights, and for another six nights after that, while the driver was away on an assignment, twenty nervous airmen earnestly asked to be rehoused, and their request was granted. Six officers then volunteered to sleep in the haunted hut, and they, too, heard the sounds and saw the evidence, but now the footprints not only led from the door to what had been the driver's bed, but then continued, passing up and down the hut as though the ghost were searching, before returning to the door. At this, the hut was sealed until a team of psychical researchers, armed with cameras, thermometers and microphones, arrived from London, and spent three nights on site. Whatever their investigation showed was not made known, at least not to Fisher. All he knows is that he saw the footprints in the hut.

As for the test-pilot's driver, he had no visitations while away on his assignment, nor when he was posted to another unit after his return to Boscombe Down.

The next story from David Bannister's file concerns an RAF pilot, John Molesworth, who completed his first tour of operations with No. 77 Squadron, based at Driffield in East Yorkshire, flying Armstrong Whitworth Whitley twin-engined bombers. In 1941, rested from combat, or "screened", as it was known, he was posted as a flying instructor to the OTU at Kinloss, on the southern bank of the Moray Firth in Scotland. His old squadron, meanwhile, had moved to Leeming in North Yorkshire, and the crews were in the process of converting from the obsolescent Whitley to the new four-engined Handley-Page Halifax. When one of the OTU's Whitleys needed a new WT set (of which there were a number going spare at Leeming), Molesworth was glad of the chance to fly the aircraft down there and renew some old acquaintances.

It so happened that, while he was waiting for the radio to be fitted, an air test for a Halifax fell due. Molesworth was eager for a trip in the big, new bomber, and his request to fly as second pilot was readily approved. It was a damp, misty day, with visibility on the airfield no better than 200 yards, and when, by an appalling miscalculation, the sergeant who was flying Molesworth's aircraft and the pilot of another Halifax both commenced their take-off runs on different, intersecting runways, a terrible collision was certain to occur.

The impact speed was 100 mph and both aircraft were totally destroyed. Men were dead and seriously injured. Sitting beside Molesworth, the sergeant pilot was sliced in half by one of the other aircraft's propellors, which, still turning at maximum speed, hit Molesworth in three places

and fractured his skull. It was a miracle that his life was spared.

It was many months before Molesworth was released from hospital and, after a period of convalescence, was able to return to his duties at Kinloss. There, he was approached by the Flying Control officer, who told him an extraordinary story. It seemed that, at the very moment of the accident at Leeming, a radio distress message, using the call-sign of the Whitley he had flown there, had been received and logged in the watch-tower at Kinloss. It was thought that he had somehow gone down in the North Sea. A full alert had been called and a sea search mounted, but nothing had been found.

In due course, John Molesworth returned to combat duties. He commanded No. 626 Squadron at Wickenby for the last eight months of the war, and retired from the RAF as Wing Commander Molesworth, DSO DFC AFC.

The men who flew the Handley-Page Halifax in World War II would never hear a word against it. For them, it was always the best of aeroplanes. I flew the Halifax myself as an instructor between tours, and found it stable, rugged and dependable. I liked it well enough, but I was glad that I flew the Lancaster on operations. Where the Lancaster was light on the controls, the Halifax was not; where the Lancaster was shapely, the Halifax was not: where the Lancaster would climb to 20,000 feet with a full load of bombs, the Merlin-engined Halifax would not. As for the cockpit panel lay-out in the Halifax, the basic instruments were in the standard pattern, but the rest might have been

thrown in through the window and fixed in where they struck. The levers for the wheels, flap and pilot's seat operated in the natural sense – up for up and down for down – but the bomb-door lever did not. I sometimes wondered how many Halifax pilots, hearing "Bombs gone" as they flew over the target, tried to close the bomb-doors, but lowered the wheels or the flaps – or the seat – instead.

In 1946, when serving at No. 11 Group Headquarters, I attended a cocktail party at Sir Frederick Handley-Page's splendid home in Stanmore. Less than completely sober and speaking face to face, I revealed my impressions of the Halifax to Sir Frederick, and drew some invidious comparisons between it and the Lancaster, while a glare of Handley-Page executives and various Air Marshals stood by. I was only rescued from that socially suicidal scene by the intervention of Sir Frederick's butler with the news that he had found another crate of bottled beer, and that if I would care to follow him…

Those inconsequential remarks are intended to serve as an introduction to the next story from the Bannister file, which concerns a Halifax pilot, Philip Fletcher. His problem was not so much with the aircraft, but with something of a different order, namely the strange circumstance he encountered on returning to his base from an operation in 1942.

During their mission, Fletcher and his crew had been engaged in a combat with a German fighter. The Halifax was damaged, but the crew had come through the combat virtually unscathed: the rear gunner's arm had been grazed by a metal fragment when the fighter's bullets put his turret out of action, and the navigator had suffered a self-inflicted injury when, sharpening a pencil, he had contrived to stab himself in the thigh. Fletcher, nursing the Halifax carefully back to northern England, found his airfield in the first dim light of morning. His aircraft was overdue, and several of his squadron colleagues, having landed earlier, were watching from the tarmac and through crew-room windows when he came into the circuit. The approach looked good – well-positioned on "finals", with the right rate of descent, the speed correct, and all lined up for landing. The watchers were amazed when Fletcher, almost at the touch-down point, suddenly applied full power and harshly wrenched the aircraft into a climbing turn.

There seemed to have been no reason for the last-minute overshoot, and the men on the ground watched anxiously while the aircraft made another circuit and another good approach. This time, however, it touched down smoothly on the runway centre line. Later, when Fletcher's colleagues asked him what had caused him to abandon his first

attempt to land, he merely said that his approach had been "all wrong", and seemed unwilling to elaborate on that. His friends were puzzled: they had seen themselves that the approach was perfect. However, they knew that Fletcher was a first-class pilot, and that he must have good reason for the overshoot. And, in a way, he did.

Looking forward through the cockpit window when he was far down the approach path, with the flap down, the speed low, and almost committed to the landing, he had been confronted with an extraordinary scene. Directly ahead of him, where the runway should have been, lay a suburban street, lined on each side with neat, semi-detached houses. Children were playing in front of the houses, and it was the sight of them that told him, whatever the danger to his aircraft and his crew, he must abort the landing. Fletcher asked his crew to say nothing of the incident until they had a chance to talk it through themselves. If all that he had seen were an illusion, it might have been that his eyes or his mind were playing tricks with him, and that could have led to medical tests and the possibility of being grounded. He was relieved to discover that, apart from the wireless operator, who was busy at the set, the rest of the crew had seen the street-scene, too. One spoke of a man who was watering his garden, another of the motor-cars that stood gleaming in the drive-ways. That was another curious thing: they had all noticed that the scene was bathed in sunlight, although the sun had not yet risen. They decided to keep the vision to themselves.

Only three of the crew survived the war. Fletcher was one of them and, thirty-six years later, as the senior sales manager of a commercial company, he attended a conference at an hotel in the north of England. The meeting ended at lunchtime on a Friday, and he looked forward to an unhurried, quiet drive home. Realising that his route passed near to his old airfield, he let nostalgia be his guide. As so often, the result was disappointing. Nothing he remembered had remained, not even the control tower, which was usually the building most likely to survive. A large part of the area had become a suburban housing estate. At last, he recognised a church spire and, from that, calculated where the main runway used to be. It was now the main street of the new estate. Furthermore, he realised, it was the very street that he and his crew had seen from their damaged Halifax in 1942.

With his mind in a turmoil, he drove to the pub he remembered from the war days and, making his way into the crowded bar, bought himself a drink and found a seat at a corner table. He was still deep in thought when a man dressed in overalls joined him at the table and, after the obligatory period of silence, asked if he were a newcomer to the neighbourhood or just passing through. Fletcher revealed his reason for being there, at which his companion asked if it were true that a Lancaster, returning from Germany, had crashed there, with the death of all the crew. The reason for his question, he went on to explain, was that some residents of the new estate claimed that, at dawn, they had heard a heavy aircraft flying overhead, and that the sound of the engines had abruptly ceased.

"Are you sure," asked Fletcher, "that it was a Lancaster?"

The man was confident it was, but Fletcher was inclined to doubt him. That ghostly sound could have been his Halifax, with four of his crewmen still aboard. It was with this thought that he bade the man good day, and resumed a thoughtful journey home.

Ability, conscientiousness and personality – those were the traits that had enabled Bob Sinclair to attain the rank of Sergeant in just over two years since his enlistment in the RAF in 1942. At RAF Binbrook, in 1944, the armourers knew him to be a fair but demanding NCO. "Check, double check, and check again" was the theme he constantly impressed upon the men who loaded high explosive into the bomb-bays of the mighty Lancasters. So it was a dreadful day for Sergeant Sinclair when he realised that, under his supervision, one whole bomb-load had been loaded live.

500lb bombs ready for loading into a Lancaster bomber 1944

He ran to the runway faster than he had ever run before, and upwind as far as he could go. Desperately he signalled, desperately he shouted, and all to no avail. As the doomed Lancaster lifted off the runway and soared above his head, the bomb-load exploded. He, and all the crew, were killed.

A few days later, it was reported that a man had been observed to be standing on the runway, waving his arms above his head. The same apparition was seen a month later, and then no more, for over a decade.

In 1956, John Sinclair (who, so far as he knew, was no relation of the Sergeant), was attending a course of training at RAF Binbrook. On his first night in residence, he took a stroll on the airfield before he went to bed. When his eyes turned towards the skyline, he saw a silhouetted figure, with arms waving wildly. His immediate thought was that someone was in trouble, and he ran towards the figure to give what help he could, but as he approached the figure disappeared.

Next evening, another member of the training course had a similar experience. He returned to the class-room to muster some support, and half-a-dozen trainees followed him out onto the runway. Again they saw the figure, again it disappeared. There was some discussion in the morning, and the trainees came to the conclusion that they had seen a wartime airman's ghost. Later, when the unit records were examined, the circumstances of the Sergeant armourer's death, and how it had happened, were revealed.

When John Sinclair heard the story, he returned to Binbrook and, at the same time in the evening as when he first saw the ghost, took up the same position on the airfield. For two evenings he saw nothing; then, on the third, there was the figure, standing on the runway, waving as madly as before. John cupped his hands round his mouth and shouted "Are you all right?"

The figure stood quite still and John called again: "Are you Sergeant Sinclair?" For a few seconds, the figure remained motionless. Then, it vanished from John's sight and there is no evidence that it was ever seen again.

See You at Breakfast

The longest and bloodiest confrontation between the RAF's Bomber Command and the enemy's air defences, later to be known as the Battle of Berlin, lasted from mid-November 1943 to the beginning of February 1944. The German capital had been attacked before, and would be again, but on fourteen nights in those eleven weeks Air Chief Marshal Harris's force flew over seven thousand sorties in an effort to destroy it. Three hundred and eighty-four bombers were lost in the battle and many more were badly damaged. My crew and I flew seven of those missions, and I know how lucky we were to survive. Of the event described in this chapter, I knew something at the time, and I was able to find one man who knew more. This, with only minor amendments, is the story as he remembers it.

"When Butch Harris launched the Battle of Berlin, Maurice Cooper's crew had been flying with the Squadron for about five months. They had taken part in attacks on many different targets, mostly deep into the heart of Germany; they had been shot up twice by night-fighters and several times by flak, they had struggled through the searchlights and a lot of nasty weather, and they had always reached the target more or less on schedule; what was more, they had sometimes hit the aiming-point. The tough trips had been very tough, and the so-called easy ones had never been that easy. Now, they were nearly at the end of their allotted tour.

On the night before the event I shall describe,

22nd November, they had flown their twenty-ninth mission, along with another 752 four-engined bombers and a few Mosquitoes, in what, up to that time, had been the heaviest attack on Hitler's capital. The city had been blanketed in cloud, as it often was that winter, but the PFF marking by radar had been good and the bombing was reasonably accurate. Poor visibility had grounded most of the night-fighters, and their absence from the arena accounted for the relatively light losses of twenty-six heavies over Europe.

Cooper had landed in the early morning, hungry, mentally exhausted and physically pooped. He had flown most of the homeward route in heavy cloud – a task made no easier by the fact that the pitot tube which provided the reading for his airspeed indicator had been iced up all the way. Two other Lancasters, whose pilots may have been in similar difficulties or worse, had crashed in England on return. Cooper and his crew had gone through the routine of de-briefing, eaten their egg-and-bacon breakfast (mandatory for bomber crews, rare for the rest of us), and tramped the half-mile to their respective Nissen huts and bed. There, with the sound of Merlin engines still ringing in their ears, with the flicker of the searchlights and the flak-shells still imprinted on their retinas, and the mingled tastes of oxygen, chewing gum, and the Padre's tot of rum lingering on their palates, they slept as best they could.

At this point, it will be as well to reveal my small involvement in the story of the crew, and to describe the situation in which they found themselves. My name is Elkington, and I was a 'penguin' or a 'wingless wonder', in what was called the Administrative and Special Duty Branch, acting as an Adjutant. Along with all the paper work, and the routine admin, I saw it as my duty (and indeed my privilege) to get to know the flying men, and to give what help I could when they had any problems.

As for Cooper's crew, their position was like this: at that time in the bomber campaign, rather less than one in five Squadron crews was finishing a tour of thirty operations: of any other four crews, most of them were dead, a few were prisoners-of-war, and a very few were attempting to evade capture somewhere in Europe. In view of these statistics, it was surprising that morale remained so high. Nevertheless, there was a general feeling that it might be lifted higher if any crew skilled enough, and fortunate enough, to complete twenty-nine missions were given a good chance to survive the last. For this, if possible, they should be despatched, not to a distant, highly hostile target, deep inside the Third Reich, but to somewhere on the fringes, on the German coast or in Occupied France, where the odds against returning were significantly reduced. This benevolent policy was never made official, but it became, at least for a while, unwritten squadron doctrine.

So it was that Cooper, waking in his hut on 23rd November, was surprised, if not to say dismayed, to be informed that he and his crew were on the Battle Order for that night, and to learn along the grape-vine that the bomb and fuel loads were the same as for the night before.

Although Cooper knew well enough that the Commander-in-Chief was determined to employ the long nights of the winter in laying waste to Berlin from end to end, he had been pinning his hopes on that unwritten rule.

When I went into the crew-room, later that morning, Cooper was standing at the window, gazing out into the distance, past the hangar on the far side of the field, past the bombers crouched on their dispersals, to where Lincoln Cathedral stood high above the farmland, twelve miles to the south. He was smoking a cigarette and seemed to be muttering to himself. His navigator strolled into the room, whistling, and stood beside him. "It'll be all right, Maurice," he said. "This time tomorrow, we'll be away on our end-of-tour leave, old boy. Think of that, eh? Bags of booze, lots of popsies..." Cooper turned and frowned at him. "Sure, or we might be down in the drink, or six feet under in a suburb of Berlin, or behind the wire in a bloody Stalag Luft. You think of that, Pete."

"Hey, don't give me the creeps! We'll make it all right."

"We're not going to try," said Cooper firmly. "I'm going to have a word with Nobby. Listen, everybody else has had an easy one to finish on – Donaldson, Ethridge, Bob Salter, Alderton, the lot. Leave it to me."

He flicked his cigarette into the coke bucket and marched out. I must confess it was purely curiosity that prompted me to follow him into the Flight Commander's office. Squadron Leader Clark was sitting at his desk, cleaning the inside of his rubber oxygen mask with a wetted handkerchief. He acknowledged Cooper's

"It won't," snapped Cooper. "I'll look after my chaps. You look after me."

"That's exactly what I'm doing. Shut the door as you go out, there's a good fellow."

"That's not good enough," said Cooper grimly, and I could tell he wasn't going to let the matter drop. I also knew it was a non-productive exercise. "Excuse me, Sir," I said. "There are a couple of rather urgent welfare matters for attention...'

Cooper swung round on me. 'Shut up, you bloody pen-pusher. This is a rather urgent matter, too. This is a matter of life and bloody death.' He turned back to Clark. "Listen, Sir, if we get the chop tonight, I'm coming back, do you understand? I'm coming back to haunt you, and you'll never get a good night's sleep again." He turned towards the door.

"For God's sake," said the Flight Commander, "I couldn't take you off the battle order even if I wanted to. It's a maximum Lanc effort. Damn it, man, I'm flying myself." Cooper looked back in the doorway and spoke quietly, almost in a whisper. "Remember what I said, Sir."

"See you at briefing, Maurice – and at breakfast tomorrow."

That was how it ended.

383 Lancasters attacked Berlin that night, and

perfunctory salute with a nod, spat on his handkerchief, and continued with his task. "The answer is no," he said, "before you ask."

Cooper glared at him. "Why? You've given all the others a milk-run to finish on, what's different about us?"

Clark examined the mask, sniffed at it, and began to clip it back onto his helmet. "Look what happened to the others, young Maurice. Salter and his lads got stinko every night, Ethridge got so twitchy that I nearly had to ground him, Donaldson's mid-upper went LMF, and he had to finish with a spare bod in the top turret. I don't want that to happen to you, old sport."

Cooper's was one of the twenty that did not come back. We never knew the reason: there were no reports from other crews of seeing them going down, no distress calls to the Air-Sea Rescue Service, no news from the International Red Cross of them being identified as casualties or prisoners-of-war. They had simply disappeared. I drafted the customary letters to the next-of-kin, and the Battle of Berlin went grimly on.

A week or so later, Nobby Clark completed his own tour on a mission to Leipzig, and departed from the Squadron to join a training unit. It was over thirty years before I saw or thought of him again. In the meantime, a Squadron Association had been formed, which I had duly joined, and a fund had been set up to commission the erection of a simple stone memorial on the old airfield site in honour of all those – there were over a thousand of them – who had been killed in action while flying with the Squadrons based there in the war.

The memorial was unveiled on a Sunday afternoon in September, with lunch beforehand in what in wartime had been the Squadron pub. I knew few people there, and few remembered me, but that had to be expected with the passage of the years. I only recognised Nobby Clark because someone spoke to him by name, and I was shocked to see how he had aged. He must have been in his late fifties but, with his thin white hair, his stoop and sunken eyes, he looked more like seventy. We stood in line together for the assembly at the memorial, and I held out my hand. "Elkington," I said, "I was Adj when you were OC 'A' Flight." We shook hands, and a flicker of recognition came into his eyes.

A familiar, chilling wind sprang up and swept across the fields while the local Vicar pronounced the dedication, and we all shivered as an Air Cadet Corps band struck up with the closing hymn. Clark and I sat together in the coach that was to take us into Lincoln and, as we travelled, I could not help but enquire about his health. "A bit up and down," he said. "I'm not as well as I would like to be. Don't sleep too well, you know."

I murmured sympathetically, and he turned to look at me. "Do you remember a chap called Cooper – Maurice Cooper – who went down on his thirtieth?"

Suddenly, I remembered Cooper. I remembered the last time I had seen him, and the words that he had said. "Yes. That was terribly bad luck."

"The funny thing is, I keep seeing him in my sleep. Standing by my bed, you know, every night. Just standing there, watching me. Pretty weird, don't you think?"

"It certainly is. And rather a nuisance for you." We sat in silence for a while, while the coach moved on towards the great Cathedral. Then I asked if he had thought of mentioning the matter to a doctor.

"Heavens, no," he said. "He'd think I'd finally gone right round the bend."

It occurred to me that what he really needed was an exorcist, but I did not pursue the matter, and we parted at the station. That was the last I saw of him. In the next issue of the Squadron Association news letter, his death was recorded in the obituary column. I learned later that he died in his sleep."

Middleton St George, now Teeside Airport, as photographed in 1942

The Canadians

For the last two years and more of World War Two, the broad acres of North Yorkshire gave the space for a lot of bomber airfields, many of which were occupied by squadrons of the Royal Canadian Air Force. At the end of 1942, 37 per cent of all the pilots serving with the RAF were from Canada, Australia or New Zealand, and of those, 60 per cent were Canadians. Then, in January 1943, the people of Canada provided the men and material for a whole new bomber Group, to be designated No.6 RCAF Group. The Canadian taxpayer met the cost of maintaining the bases, and of the aircraft, the fuel, the bombs and ammunition. Nearly all the pilots, navigators, bomb-aimers, wireless-operators and gunners were Canadian, while the RAF provided most of the flight-engineers. The Group Headquarters was located in Allerton Park Castle, a Victorian mansion near Knaresborough, known to the Canadians as "Castle Dismal" for its somewhat forbidding frontage, and seven operational airfields, plus three for conversion training, were located in and beside the Vale of York and beyond it to the River Tees. At full strength, the Group consisted of

Andrew C Mynarski, VC

fifteen squadrons, equipped initially with Vickers Wellingtons, then with Handley-Page Halifaxes, which became the mainstay of the Group, and with Avro Lancasters in the last year of the war.

One of the first bases to be occupied by No.6 Group was Middleton St. George, near Darlington in County Durham, and the first units to move in there were Nos.420 (Snowy Owl) Squadron, later replaced by No.428 (Ghost) Squadron, and No.419 (Moose) Squadron. From 1943 onwards their Halifaxes, and ultimately Lancasters, played a full part in the bomber war. Their last operation was on 25th April 1945, when fifteen aircraft from each squadron attacked German gun batteries on the island of Wangeroog in the Heligoland Bight.

The Group was disbanded when the war was won, and, at the end of May 1945, the aircrew of Middleton St. George's squadrons flew home across the North Atlantic. With them they took a splendid reputation, and behind them, somewhere in Europe, they left 1,157 young Canadians who had died in action. One of the dead was Pilot Officer Andrew Charles Mynarski, a mid-upper gunner of No. 419 Squadron.

On the night of 12th June 1944, Mynarski's aircraft, the Canadian-built Lancaster KB726, while en route to attack rail communications at Cambrai, was hit and set on fire by a Junkers 88 equipped with the deadly upward-firing cannon known as Schrage Musik. The pilot gave the order to bale out – an order which the rear gunner, Flying Officer Pat Brophy, trapped in his turret, was unable to obey. Mynarski, seeing his comrade's plight, made his way aft and tried to extricate him, but the turret's mechanism was irretrievably jammed. Mynarski was severely burned in the attempt and, with the aircraft still descending and dangerously low, Brophy urgently motioned the mid-upper gunner to jump. Brophy last saw Mynarski, with his clothes ablaze, throwing up his hand in a last salute before he disappeared. Mynarski's parachute, damaged by the fire, did not develop fully, and he died of his injuries next day. Brophy, miraculously, was thrown clear of the aircraft when it crashed, and it was his subsequent testimony that brought his fellow-gunner the posthumous award of the Victoria Cross. Mynarski was buried in a village cemetery to the east of Amiens. Middleton St. George remained an active RAF airfield until April 1964, when it was acquired by the Durham County Council. It became a busy civil airfield, and in due course attained the status of Teesside International Airport. The wartime officers' mess was converted into the St. George Airport Hotel and, in 1985, the Canadian veterans returned for the dedication of a memorial cairn in the hotel garden.

There remains a strong belief locally that the spirit of Andrew Mynarski haunts the site of the old aircraft hangars and the Airport Hotel. "People who have never heard of Mynarski," Ted Stone of Middlesborough told me, "have described him perfectly, coming out of what used to be the mess."

There is, however, an alternative opinion as to the ghost's identity – or it may be there is another ghost at Middleton St. George. There is a theory that the airfield is haunted by a Canadian pilot, John McCullen, who, returning from a mission on 13th January 1945 in a badly damaged Lancaster, told his crew to use their parachutes, while he himself stayed and died at the controls in ensuring that the bomber crashed in open country. A road in the village was named for Mc Cullen, and it is he, say some, who haunts the old airfield buildings.

In 1977, the Canadian Warplane Heritage Museum at Mount Hope, Ontario, acquired a Mark X Lancaster, FM213, which had been standing on the shores of Lake Huron as an open-air exhibit for thirteen years. A group of volunteers, some 2,000 strong, set themselves the task of restoration. They called themselves the Canadian Warplane Heritage Support Group, and their long-term aim was to see FM213 fly. Ten years later, with the help of airplane builders and engineers from all over Canada, they achieved their aim. They changed the aircraft's registration from FM213 to KB726, and in September 1988, "The Mynarski Lancaster", as they named her, made her second flight. On board the aircraft, thanks to erstwhile members of the French Resistance, was the very axe with which the gallant gunner had tried to free Pat Brophy, and Brophy himself, with Mynarski's sister, was there to see the flight. Now KB726 takes part in air

Hangar 3 at Teeside.
Many on the airfield refuse to enter this hangar after dark

The memorial cairn outside the
wartime officers mess now
converted into The George
Airport Hotel

displays and national events throughout the land, in the same way that PA474, the Battle of Britain Memorial Flight's "City of Lincoln", the only other flying Lancaster, thrills and delights crowds all over Britain.

The walled city of York, with its great Minster and historic buildings, with its famous Betty's Bar, the de Grey Rooms, and many more fine hostelries, was the favourite destination, when they were on stand-down, for the thousands of young men who had come from Quebec, Ontario, Manitoba and all points west to fight the bomber war. One of the inns the fliers liked to patronise was The Golden Fleece, which stood (and still stands) on a street known as Pavement, south of the old market place between the Minster and the Merchant Venturers' Hall.

It seems that, on an evening in April 1945, a party of airmen from one of the local bases, Linton-on-Ouse perhaps, or East Moor or Tholthorpe, booked rooms at The Golden Fleece and set forth on a pub-crawl. Late that night, one of the party, waking in his third floor room and searching for the lavatory, stumbled into another bedroom, fell out of the window, through the glass roof above a passage-way, and broke his neck on landing.

It was a minor tragedy in the context of the times, but bars were fitted to that third floor window, the room was locked and put out of bounds. So much is remembered by Mrs Gloria Cartwright, whose parents took the inn over post-war. Gloria's bedroom was next to the locked one and, as she told a reporter of the Yorkshire Evening Press, she felt an un-easiness whenever she passed it, and never put her lights out when she went to bed. "I didn't see anything," she said, "but I knew there was something there, and I was scared. It was as though something or somebody was watching me." Gloria recalls that a quartet of stage acrobats, staying at the inn while fulfilling an engagement at what was then the Empire Theatre, were so shaken by the ambience that they passed the night huddled together in a single room and checked out in the morning.

The next development came when the Keenan family from Quincy, Northern California, holidaying in England at Easter in 1994, spent a dark and windy Saturday night at The Golden Fleece. Shortly after midnight, Mrs. Keenan – and

it so happened that her name was April – was awakened by something, or someone, pulling at her hair. As she lay there, afraid but unresisting, hands touched her arms and then her feet. She and her husband had little further sleep and, when the landlady, Mrs Sally Pyne, noticed their obvious signs of agitation in the morning, they told her what had happened. The Keenans returned to California, convinced that April had been in contact with a ghost.

Three months later, when Mrs. Pyne had almost put the matter out of mind, April Keenan called her on the transatlantic telephone, and told her that The Golden Fleece's ghost was now with her in Quincy. "He's making my life a misery," she said, "and I can't think what to do. He says he's a Canadian airman who died in the war at your hotel. Last Friday morning, I woke up and found I'd written "Geoff Monk died at The Golden Fleece" on a piece of paper by my bed."

"I'm ever so sorry, love," said Mrs. Pyne, "but I don't know how I can help."

"I thought, if I could find out whether what he says is true, I might find some way of putting him at rest."

Appraised of the problem by the Evening Press, a local group of students of the paranormal held a seance, at which they received the information that the wandering spirit's name was Geoff Monroe, that he had died on 25th April 1945, that he came from Saskatchewan – and that he wanted to go back there. Later, through their contact on "the other side" they had a brief question and answer session with Geoff Monroe's spirit. In itself, this was unproductive, but their

feeling was that they had persuaded him to "walk into the light", and that Mrs. Keenan's problems might be at an end. Mrs. Betty Petre, however, who, as a child, had delivered bread to the hotel, and felt an interest in the matter, took a different view. "I'm sure," she said, "that if Mrs. Keenan were to take a trip across the border into Canada, she would be free of the ghost forever."

It did not come to that. The last that Sally Pyne heard from California was that the Keenans were at peace. It seemed that either the efforts of the York group had been rewarded, or that another, higher agency had prevailed. One way or another, Geoff Monroe had walked into the light.

In addition to providing a whole RCAF bomber group in northern England, Canada sent thousands of her sons to fly and fight with RAF squadrons in the other groups of Air Chief Marshal Harris's Command. One of these young Canadians was Willis Quigley, who sent me the following story from his home in Halifax, Nova Scotia. In 1943, he crossed the Atlantic in the Queen Elizabeth and, at OTU, joined a newly-formed bomber crew as the rear gunner. Brian Little, the navigator, was a commissioned officer, but Bert Cooper, the pilot, and the other members of the crew, including Quigley and another Canadian, were NCOs. When their training was completed, they were posted to a No. 5 Group squadron, No. 61, based at Skellingthorpe, a few miles west of Lincoln. They began their tour of operations and, as Quigley described it: "Although we were all well-trained and had participated in exercises, I must say we viewed our first operational trip with some trepid-

ation. Now we were venturing into enemy territory, a different world; the games were over, the enemy was using real bullets. It was similar, I am sure, to entering a jungle which one knew to be full of snakes and tigers, where an attack was to be expected at any time." The crew were very close, as good crews always were, and Quigley especially enjoyed the company of the navigator, Brian Little. It was for Brian's nephew, Adrian, that Quigley composed his recollections of their days together, in the air and on the ground, and it is from that document that I have taken these extracts. Some have nothing at all to do with ghosts, but they provide a cogent record of the times, and of the sort of man that Quigley was.

"The atmosphere on the Squadron was happy-go-lucky, although after a long, difficult flight everyone was tired; they were resilient and, after some sleep, were ready and set to fly again or, if flying was not scheduled, or cancelled due to weather, to go to the pubs and have an evening of fun. Thank God for the English pub and fish and chips. The civilian population, whose lives were also stressful, derived the same benefits as we did. They were very supportive of our efforts. We got to know them, drink, eat, play darts and generally have fun with them. When I look back on that experience, I realise they were surrogate families to us."

On the night of 26/27th May 1944, Quigley had a dream: "It was very short, like a snapshot, lasting only seconds. My grandfather had died before I joined the Air Force, but he appeared in my dream. I could only see his face, which seemed very red. He did not speak, but from his expression, I knew he was warning me of something."

The next night, Quigley's crew set out on their thirteenth operation, joining a force of 100 Lancasters and 4 Mosquitoes of No. 5 Group in an attack on workshops and a railway junction in the town of Nantes, on the western coast of France, where the river Loire flows into the Atlantic. The first fifty bomb-loads to fall on the target were so accurately aimed that the Master Bomber called a halt to the attack, and instructed the remainder of the force to save their bombs for somewhere else. One Lancaster only failed to return to base, but Quigley's aircraft did not escape unscathed.

"We encountered searchlights, heavy anti-aircraft fire and an attack by an Me-210. An instant before it fired at us, the dream flashed through my mind, and almost involuntarily I wheeled the turret round and pointed the guns downward, yelling to Bert to make a diving turn to port. The fighter's guns damaged our plane, raking the tail-planes and the aft top and under ends of the fuselage. Several bullets hit the rear turret, badly damaging one of my gun-barrels while I was firing back, but I got a burst away with both guns as the Me-210 flashed upwards behind us, and saw some tracer rake the front under part of its fuselage. Then one barrel became white hot, and I had to put it on the safety position to prevent it from firing. I was slightly hurt, with a bullet crease on my temple.

Our aircraft, which was already in a diving turn, was now screaming earthward. When Bert managed to pull out of the dive, we were about 100 feet above the ground, and I was staring down the chimney flues of houses below us. When we got back to England it was daylight; we looked at the aircraft, and could hardly believe our eyes.

Tail-planes and rudders had been virtually shot away, and the rear turret looked like a sieve."

Quigley's tour ended prematurely on 6/7th June 1944, when his Lancaster was attacked on a daylight operation by a pair of Focke-Wulf 190s. Quigley was seriously injured, and was lucky not to lose a leg, if not his life. Four months later, he was on his feet again and walking with a stick, but his flying days were over. His crew, meanwhile, with a replacement rear gunner, continued with their tour until, on their twenty-sixth mission, they were once again attacked, and this time they did not return. After further surgery in Canada, Quigley married the girl he had left behind in Halifax when he had sailed for England, and, reverting to his trade of electrical engineering, enlisted in the Canadian Navy, with which service he continued to serve in a civilian capacity until his retirement in 1993. He still believes that a waking dream once saved his life.

The Yellow Scarf

The story which provides the title for this chapter was contributed by Rex Polendine, who lives at Sleaford, Lincolnshire, in the heart of bomber country.

"As it had been with many of my age-group in the war years, the time-span between school days and enlistment was brief, and while old school friends tried to keep in touch, any contact was limited to chance meetings when on leave. Everyone then set course for the hostelry where we had experienced our baptism of near-beer.

Three of us managed to get together at fairly regular intervals, and our bond of friendship increased over that period. We were of mixed temperament. One, a fearless chap who romped through training and bomber operations, and was quite unperturbed when an extra six  ops were tacked on to the end of his tour. Not sharing his conviction of immortality, I was frequently frightened and knew that I was of less heroic mould; nevertheless, I was still happy to shoot my quota of lines. The third member of our small band was different – a quiet, gentle person and very unwarlike in demeanour and speech. He was the one who 'failed to return'.

Needless to say, news of his loss was felt deeply, but as details were confined to the usual 'missing' telegram to his family, we hoped for the best. For some reason, I was convinced that he would survive, even after his death was confirmed when the war ended. By then, other well-known faces were missing from our habitual meeting place, but we had become hardened to the mounting casualties, and it was only in later years that we gave less self-centred thoughts to those who did not survive.

There was certain amount of readjustment on return to civilian life, and although friendships endured, priorities had to be centred on a more down-to-earth existence. Bar-room badinage between wartime buddies was maintained, but a number of years passed before our journeys of pilgrimage commenced.

A couple of car-loads were involved in the initial trips, which were confined to the airfields from where one or more of the party had operated. As the years passed, the numbers decreased and eventually dwindled to myself and the second survivor of our wartime trio, plus another ex-Lancaster lad we had both known in our school-days. Many of the old bases were returning to the plough, and farm machinery dominated the scene on weed-encrusted concrete and in the weather-beaten buildings. This did not detract from the nostalgic atmosphere, and it was easy to imagine the sound of an engine run-up from a far-off dispersal – and there was the well-remembered

Lincolnshire breeze to chill the bones…

For a long time we neglected to visit the base from which our lost friend had flown on his last operation. Indeed, we had shamefully forgotten the date, and in an effort to ascertain this we at last made for the Wolds and the remnants of his airfield, with a vague feeling that the information would be forthcoming there.

On site, little was visible of the station, only a few sagging huts and scattered areas of decaying peri-track. But we did locate the pub. There was always one within staggering distance of an RAF base, and this one was unchanged from the war years. Unlike those days, we found the rooms empty with the exception of the landlord, who welcomed us cordially and provided a bar snack with draughts of good bitter. On hearing of our interest in the locality, he directed us to the room that had been the aircrew haven, and left us to enjoy our meal. We were rather puzzled that the place was so empty, but assumed that lunch time was not a busy period. It gave us freedom to explore the room and try to envisage how it would have been crowded with noisy airmen so many years before.

There was certainly evidence of wartime occupation amongst the battle-scarred tables and chairs. We sat at a table near the bar, and scrutinised it closely in the hope of finding our friend's initials scratched among those faintly discernible on the polished surface. This was doubtful, as he had not been on the squadron long and, in any case, was not the type to disfigure furniture.

We stayed for little more than an hour, and paused before departing for a last word with the landlord. He informed us that the adjacent church contained a roll of honour on which the names of squadron casualties were recorded. This was unexpected gen which could provide the answer to our quest. We thanked the landlord, and made our way to the church. The roll of honour was impressive, elaborately bound in blue and gold covers, and housed in a glass case. The multitude of names covering the parchment leaves conveyed their own sad story, and it was a subdued trio that scanned them, looking for just one entry. It was there – name, number and date – a bleak and final confirmation. We stood for some minutes, each lost in his own thoughts. Although it was a warm day, the air seemed colder than when we entered.

At last we closed the book and made for the door. On the step we were surprised to meet our helpful landlord. 'I thought I might catch you,' he said. 'You left this behind on your table.' He held out a yellow scarf. We thanked him for his trouble, but said we could lay no claim to the article.

The landlord appeared reluctant to accept this, and at his insistence we examined it; it was just an ordinary silk scarf, rather old-fashioned, and certainly not our property. Handing it back, we asked why he was so sure it belonged to one of us. He explained that he had cleaned the room in which we had lunched, and that no-one else had been in there before we arrived or after we left. "If it's not yours," he asked, "who left it there?"

We had no answer to that, but his sincerity caused us all to voice the same question as we headed for the car-park. Sitting in the car, we looked across the ploughed land that thirty years before had been bisected by the tyre-scarred main runway. One of us ventured a thought. "If you remember, we all had a similar sort of scarf in those days." It was not necessary to elaborate. We were on the same wave-length – the rather tatty bits of silk, of odd colours and sizes, tied around our necks under battle-dress collars or stuffed under aircrew sweaters. They gave no great warmth, but were greatly cherished and protected from thievery at all costs – an aircrew fetish.

As we set course for home, we pondered the significance of our experience. None of us was of an imaginative nature, but we had to admit the episode had created a strange sense of unreality. The facts could not be denied and the questions remained. The airfield had been closed for many years, and the pub unused by aircrew for the same period. The landlord had been convinced that piece of silk belonged to one of us, and had seemed disturbed when we failed to acknowledge it. As he had said, there had been no-one there, except our trio.

Or had there been a fourth visitor, unseen by all of us?"

As a postscript to his story, Rex Polendine told me that, within a few days of the episode of the yellow scarf, another veteran had visited that same village church, and had experienced something of a shock when he found his own name, rank and number among those inscribed upon the roll of honour.

A story with some similarities to Rex Polendine's was told by Mrs. Olive Rowley, ne Brown, who lives not far from Uttoxeter in Derbyshire. I recorded it on a tape-recorder at her home, and I have edited it slightly, to exclude some repetitions and the occasional interruption from her children, but this is basically what she said.

"In those days, in 1967, when this odd thing happened, I used to do early evenings in the bar at The Hollybush. Nice, quiet village pub, and Dad knew the licensee, so he didn't mind me working there. One evening that September, I'd just opened up when these four lads came in. Well, young men, really – late teens, early twenties. They weren't local, I could tell, because I knew all the village boys – you know what I mean – knew them all by sight, and I hadn't heard a car or any motor-bikes outside, so I thought they might be from the College, out hiking or something. One of them, a tall chap, ever so good-looking, came up to the bar and asked if I served pints. I said that was what I was there for, and he smiled and ordered four jars of the best bitter. He asked me if I'd have something myself, and I said I'd have a Britvic orange, thank you very much.

He asked what that was, and I showed him the bottle. He looked at it and asked if it was nice, and

'An aeroplane called the Wellington…'

I said it was. "Well, you enjoy it, miss," he said. "By the way," he went on, "we'll probably have two or three more, so keep a count, will you, and we'll settle up when we leave."

That was a bit out of the way, but they seemed respectable enough. I mean, I'd had a good look at them, the way you get used to doing in the bar-trade. Short haircuts, polished shoes, one in a raincoat, two in high-neck pullovers, and the tall one who ordered the beer was in a nice leather jacket. They sat up at the bar, and the boy in the raincoat took a couple of dice out of his pocket, and they played some sort of game with them. 'Liar dice', they called it. I couldn't understand it, but they seemed to get a lot of fun out of it.

They had another round of drinks, and one of them sat down at the old piano in the corner and began to play a tune. It was an old one, 'In the mood'. He played really well. Then the one in the raincoat asked if Fred Wright was still around. I said "If you mean Mr. Wright that used to keep the garage across from the Post Office, I'm afraid he passed away a few years ago. His son's still there, though."

One of the others said "What about the village bobby, Les Brown?"

I said: "Well, my name's Brown, and my Uncle Les was the policeman here, years back. But I wouldn't have thought you were old enough to know him." He smiled, and said: "Perhaps we're a bit older than we look, miss. He was a good type, your Uncle. Kept us out of trouble once or twice, didn't he, you chaps?"

They all agreed, and they had another round, which I wrote down as before. Then they went back

to the piano, and the one who could play struck up with 'Bless 'em all' – I hadn't heard that since I was little – and they all sang the words.

'Bless 'em all, bless 'em all,
The long and the short and the tall,
Bless all the Sergeants and WO1s,
Bless all the Corporals and their blinking sons,
For we're saying goodbye to them all,
As back to their billets they crawl,
You'll get no promotion this side of the ocean,
So cheer up, my lads, bless 'em all!'

They were still singing when the phone rang, and I went into the hall to answer it. The caller asked if this was The Hollybush, and if there were four men there. I said it was, and yes, they were. He said he thought there would be, and he was coming to join them, but he'd got into a traffic snarl-up outside Birmingham. He said: "Will you let them know I'm on my way?" I asked him for his name, and he said: "Just say Tail-end Charlie".

Well, I might have known it. I could hear them singing while I was on the phone, but were they there when I went back in the bar? No, they were not. I ran out the back (because I knew they hadn't gone out past me in the hall), and peeped into the loo, which was outside in the yard, but there wasn't a sign of them. And yet they'd seemed so nice.

I found a note in pencil on the bar when I went back in. It read "Tell your Uncle the lads from hut 13 were asking after him. Thanks, and goodbye." While I was reading that, a couple of my regulars came in. They bought a couple of halves, and sat down to their dominoes. All I could think of was

how I was going to explain twelve pints out of the barrel and no money in the till. I'd quite forgotten about the chap who had phoned until he turned up about twenty minutes later. He stared around the bar, and said "Oh, no, don't tell me they've gone!" I told him they must have left while he was on the phone. He sat down at the bar, and put his head down in his hands. He looked so upset I hadn't the heart to say anything about the drinks. Then he lifted his head and said "How did they look? Did they seem all right?"

"Well, yes, they did," I said. "They had a good sing at the piano. And a few drinks, as a matter of fact, that they forgot to pay for."

He took out a wallet and gave me a tenner. It occurred to me that perhaps I'd been right about them being College boys, and perhaps this chap was their tutor or something. I mean, he was a lot older than they were. When I brought his change, he said "You keep that, my dear, for looking after them while they were here." I couldn't help asking who they were. "It's a bit difficult to explain," he said.

"Try me," I said. Yes, I know I'm cheeky.

"Well, we used to fly together. We were the crew of an aeroplane called the Wellington. You won't have heard of that."

"Yes, I have," I said. "My Dad told me about them. There were some based a few miles away. Excuse me for saying this, you might be old enough for that, but the lads who were here were much too young to have been flying then."

He wasn't listening, just looking at me without really seeing me, if you know what I mean. "We used to come here," he said, "to this pub. Like brothers, we were. We always had a lot of fun. We made a promise that, if anything happened, we'd meet here twenty-five years later to the day. This is the day."

He stopped, and I took two halves round to the domino table. Then I went back behind the bar. "Go on," I said, quietly, "what did happen?"

"There was a crash on take-off. Starboard engine failure. I was the rear gunner, and my turret was thrown clear. I was the only survivor."

Anthony Leicester
at the controls of a Wellington

Turn Back! Turn Back!

Anthony Leicester

As darkness settled over the steaming Bengal jungle, I followed my crew up the ladder and climbed into the nose of our Wellington bomber. We cursed our bulky flying jackets, parachute harnesses and Mae Wests. Sweat soaked our khaki shirts, further irritating the prickly heat that plagued us all.

We were with 215 Squadron stationed at Jessore, Bengal, where the greatest hazards we faced were monsoon thunderstorms, heat, humidity, mechanical problems and dysentery – not night fighters, searchlights and ack-ack that flooded the skies over Europe.

Before starting the engines I called to the crew, "Give me an intercom check."

Mac sitting behind his four Browning machine guns answered first. "Rear gunner O.K., Skipper."

Fane, the radio operator, and Frank, the navigator in the cabin behind the cockpit spoke almost simultaneously.

"Ready, Skipper."

My bomb aimer, Nick Rushton, settled into the auxiliary seat beside me and gave me a thumbs up sign.

The five of us had been flying together for nearly a year, a long time by World War II standards. Although the youngest of the crew, aged twenty, I was their skipper.

It was the night of January 26, 1944, we were setting out on an operational sortie to bomb the railway marshaling yards at Mandalay east of the Arakan hills. We'd been told in the briefing to look for the hooded-lights of Japanese trucks on jungle roads and, if we saw any, bomb them. The plane carried a mixed assortment of bombs having a total of 4000-pounds.

I taxied slowly toward the end of the runway, an aircraft directly ahead and another behind. The air brakes hissed as I released the pressure on the control column brake lever then, as I squeezed the handle the brake linings squealed protesting the Wellington's lumbering weight.

I turned and lined up with the runway, a single row of smouldering paraffin flare pots served as runway lights on my left. At the ops briefing I had been given a take-off time and at that precise moment I eased the throttles forward with my left hand, pushing the right lever slightly ahead to hold the ungainly aircraft straight until I had rudder control.

As the plane slid away from the wavering lights and rose into the velvet-black tropical darkness I touched the brakes to stop the wheels spinning and raised the undercarriage. The jet-black aircraft inched upward and the wheels clunked into the engine nacelles.

Inside the cockpit pale-green instrument dials glowed just enough to be visible. Outside, the two Hercules sleeve-valve engines roared like wounded animals until I throttled them back for the long slow climb to our operating altitude, heading eastward to Burma.

The sky, a black star-studded dome, blinked

and flickered like a field of diamonds. Other than an occasional routine report from one of the crew to me, or to one another, the intercom was silent.

I was leaning back in my seat with the knee rest raised under my legs, listening to the engine's steady mesmerizing beat when slowly, a strange feeling stole over me. A strange unrest I couldn't push aside. For another hour we flew on performing our respective jobs. Finally the gnawing sensation of impending danger drove me to click the microphone button and break the intercom's silence.

"Frank, give me a course for the nearest emergency landing strip" I said quietly to the navigator, "We're turning back."

It seemed ages before he answered.

"What's wrong, Skipper?" It was Fane talking from the little cubicle he shared with his Marconi radio transmitter and receiver behind me. "You have a problem up there?"

I flipped the switch. "Everything looks good on the gauges, but I've an uneasy feeling that something's wrong. We shouldn't go on."

After a long pause a sarcastic voice cut the tense silence. "Losing your nerve, Skipper?"

In the seat beside me Nick leaned forward and examined the instrument panel as if saying, what the hell's wrong anyway?

I turned on the red cockpit light and noted the tightness of his jaw and the quick movement of his scanning eyes.

Apparently satisfied with what he saw, he leaned back and glanced uneasily at me.

"Feel all right, Skipper?"

I paused.

"I'm fine, Nick, but I have a feeling," I paused, "No, a premonition we're heading for trouble."

Nick didn't answer. I tried to analyze my uneasiness but I couldn't. No gauge had flickered a warning. The steady drone of the engines hadn't sounded different. It wasn't fear; it was just a strange sensation. A sensation that there was something looming behind me. Some invisible force. A sensation I'd had before but couldn't remember when.

I spoke to the navigator again. "Frank. Give me that heading to Chittagong. We're turning back."

When he answered I eased the control column over, leveled the wings and settled the aircraft on the compass course he'd given me.

The intercom fell silent. I sensed the crew's hostility. I knew they were perturbed by my decision. Did they think I'd lost my nerve? ...or feared enemy fighters? ...or were they remembering the bad crash we had during training back home at OTU? That one at Chipping Warden had been partially my fault, but they had never before questioned my decisions.

How could I explain to them the force that made me turn back? The engines drummed steadily as I tried to think where I had experienced the odd sensation before.

Suddenly it came to me. I was a little boy in Weybridge. I had just put my bicycle away in the

The Wellington cockpit

wooden shed at the end of the garden. It was autumn, late in the afternoon and nearly dark. As I turned to leave the shed, a strange feeling made me stand perfectly still. It was if icy fingers had touched my skin. Was someone, or something behind me in that dark shed?

Afraid to look back I bolted through the door, and flew over the gravel path as fast as my little legs would move me to the safety of the lighted house.

The same sensation of impending danger had prompted my order to turn back.

Ahead on the ground a few dim lights appeared. Small outdoor fires in the village of Chittagong, a native village on the edge of the Bay of Bengal near the mouth of the river Ganges.

As I descended, looking for the landing strip cut into the jungle, I called across to Nick. "We'll drop the bombs, safe, on the beach over there."

Turning the plane towards the beach I could see the white surf breaking on the sand. Nick slid from his seat to the bomb aimer's position below me.

I moved the lever to open the bomb doors and called over the intercom. "Bomb doors open. Drop 'em when you're ready."

A moment later the aircraft lurched as 4000 pounds of bombs fell through the open bomb-bay doors. The sudden unexpected huge orange flash of exploding bombs gave me a fleeting glimpse of land, sea and clouds, then blackness.

"What the hell happened, Nick?"

"Don't know," leaving his bombsight he climbed back into his seat beside me. "I left the switch on

'safe' but they all went off anyway." He shook his head, "Lucky they missed the beach. Looked as if they hit the ocean some distance out."

I turned my attention to the landing. We were on final approach and there were no runway lights. I would have to get the aircraft down without any help from the ground.

As I skimmed over the trees at the end of the narrow landing strip I closed the throttles and yellow flames spurted from the short exhaust stacks. Tyres squealed on the tarmac; it was a good landing but the crew's usual ribald comments were missing.

I glanced at Nick beside me. He was looking straight ahead, his face a sullen mask.

Ahead, near a small thatched bamboo building, a torch's wavering light appeared. I taxied slowly towards it until a side-to-side movement signaled me to stop. The hatch was opened from outside and a hand reached in to pull down the wooden ladder. No-one spoke.

Quickly undoing my seat belt and shoulder harness, I was first to step on the tarmac. I saw the double stripes on a corporal's shirtsleeve.

"God! You're lucky you made it, Sarge," he said, flashing his torch on the left side of the aircraft.

Instead of dull black paint, the Wellington's fuselage glistened with globules of oil running down and dripping on to the ground. One by one my crew came down the ladder, stood beside me and stared silently at the shiny black slime.

The cooling engines creaked and crackled. Then, from on top of the engine's nacelle, a voice called. "I checked the oil, Skipper. You had about ten-minutes flying left before the bloody engine seized solid. There's a ton of metal in the filter. Looks like the bearings have had it."

Suddenly the crew were talking among themselves. The corporal moved close beside me, "Did you see the fighters parked alongside the runway?" he asked.

"What fighters?"

"Over there." He pointed his torch. I walked along the light's path. Sure enough, eight Spitfires were lined up wingtip to wingtip. With their wheels on the edge of the landing strip the fighter's long Merlin engines stretched several feet out over the runway.

Those icy fingers touched me again. I couldn't believe I had landed without my wingtip ripping into the marshaled aircraft.

From behind, I heard flight-boots shuffling towards me.

"Thanks, Skipper." a voice said softly.

A hand squeezed my arm, "Keep that crystal ball polished Tony, we'll take it along on all our flights."

Building the terminal and control tower at Speke

Captain Black

Jeremy M Pratt

The legend of Captain Black is older even than the now empty 1939 terminal and control tower that dominate the original 'Speke' airfield site. It is a legend in which I, unknowingly, played a walk-on role.

I've always had a soft spot for Liverpool airport. In truth, it's not the most picturesque of airfields, not even with the smoke-belching chimneys of the nearby oil refineries reflected off the greasy waters of the Mersey estuary. For sure, Liverpool (or Speke, as it used to be known) is no green English airfield, with grass runways and twee hangars nestling in rolling hills and woodland. However, I did a lot of my training there, firstly flying solo circuits and cross-countries when I was getting my PPL, and subsequently when Dennis Dickinson taught me the art of flying (and surviving) as a Flying Instructor. In later years, I returned to Liverpool to fly for Dennis, trying to pass on the finer points of aeronautical craft to young and impressionable apprentice fighter pilots, delivered to us courtesy of the Air Training Corps and an RAF Scholarship scheme. When you spend a lot of time flying from one airfield, you do tend to develop a fondness for it. Its familiarity and your intimate knowledge of all its quirks makes it some sort of safe haven. Once you are confident of your ability to return safely to those friendly runways, even in the worst conditions, there is a homeliness about the place that stays with you. I guess many pilots could say the same for their own 'home' airfield.

And yet, there was something about the old airfield that made me inexplicably uneasy. More than once, putting the aircraft away in hangar 1 after night flying, I felt a sudden urge to look over my shoulder, to get out into the bright lights on the apron. Sometimes at night, after commiserating with a fellow instructor in the bar of the old art-deco terminal, I would walk across the apron, past hangar 1, back to my car. Then I had a sense of being unsettled, without knowing why. I would walk that bit faster, and fumble my car keys in my keenness to be on my way. I never did dash out of hangar 1, nor run across the apron to my car; but I never looked over my shoulder either.

Of course, I heard the reports about phantom airmen and headless apparitions. I put these down to an unsubtle wind-up, the sort of trick that old-hands like to play on young, naive flying instructors. So I ignored these stories.

My visits to Liverpool became less frequent as the years rolled on, and I thought little more about the atmosphere I had often sensed there. Little more, that is, until one day a few months ago. I was talking to Mike Rudkin, an Air Traffic Controller at Manchester Airport who, as it happens, started his career at Liverpool.

"Did you ever come across Captain Black?" he asked as we were reminiscing about the now deserted art-deco terminal building at Liverpool, and its vintage, lighthouse-style control tower. The name meant nothing to me, until he described his own encounter with 'Captain Black'. I was so intrigued that I asked him to write the story down for me. He did, these are his words.

"I began my career in Air Traffic Control at Liverpool Airport on a cold, rain-soaked November day in 1970. I was a very green eighteen year old, but many of the Air Traffic Controllers at Liverpool at that time were ex-RAF aircrew, some of whom had wartime experience. Most had spent many years at 'Speke', as the airport was still known then.

I first heard of the eponymous Captain Black in small talk during the long night-watches in the control tower. There were, supposedly, a number of people on the airport who had seen a spectral figure on the apron, or in the 1930s hangar 1. However, I was enjoying the new-found freedoms of no parental control, public houses etc. and so I did not pursue the sightings. All I can say is that the old airfield certainly could be a scary place at night, although how much was down to youthful imagination I don't know.

The control tower was part of the original 1930s terminal, and could only be reached by a suitably ancient lift with a two-person capacity. To catch out the unwary, the lift was equipped with a heavy manual gate that had to be closed firmly on leaving, or else no-one else could call it. Any failure by a junior member of staff to secure this gate was guaranteed to earn a major rollicking, as this would mean that somebody (usually me!)

would have to locate the lift and restore it to working condition.

Night duties were very quiet, and this particular night was no exception as the gentle hum of the air-conditioning lulled me into a state of mindlessness. Suddenly there was a loud clang as the lift left the tower, having been called down. But who had summoned it? Other than ourselves there was nobody else in this portion of the building and, of course, access was secured against intruders. With an abrupt jerk the cable drums stopped turning, then there was silence. Whoever had requested the lift had not got into it – there was no sound of the doors being drawn open. Nor did the lift move on to any other floor. I reached forward and pressed the call button. Nothing. I forced a crack in the tower doors and peered down into the darkness of the lift shaft. The lift was out-of-sight, well beyond the limit of access afforded by the fire escape than ran down the outside the tower. Nothing else for it, we needed the fire service! They arrived quickly and, after obtaining the keys, found the lift in the basement – its doors wide open. The basement was an equipment room which could only be accessed from the apron, via a heavily-padlocked door. The fire service found nobody in the basement, the padlock on the access door was still in place! My colleague, Dave Wilkinson, turned to me with a look of weary resignation, 'Bloody Captain Black again'."

Inside the Speke control tower, 1939

The story got me thinking. Mike had continued to assume that 'Captain Black' was an imaginary name given to the source of the strange occurrences that continued to plague the old buildings of Liverpool Airport. A few days after Mike sent me his story, he called:

"I've found him"

"Who?"

"Captain Black. He's real – or at least he was"

Mike's call fired my imagination, and the legend began to grip me. When I moved house, a long-forgotten book with a bookmark on one particular page turned up some traces. By chance, in a second-hand bookshop I came across a copy of 'Flight' magazine from 1934. Within there was a photograph, a face to a name. On a flying school noticeboard a photocopied magazine article yielded more clues. The pieces of the jigsaw slowly came together. This is a story that has its roots in the 1930s – the golden era of flying some say.

Thomas Campbell-Black was the epitome of the dashing pioneer pilot during the era of the great record-breaking flights, in the decade before the Second World War. He flew with both the Royal Naval Air Service and

the RAF in the First World War. Post war, whilst farming in the colony of Kenya (as it then was), he became a pioneer of civil aviation in Africa and of flights between Kenya and England. He founded Wilson Airways in Nairobi, and there taught Beryl Markham to fly. They became lovers. Beryl Markham went on to be a pioneer pilot in her own right when she became the first woman to fly across the Atlantic solo, non-stop, from east to west. However, before this achievement, Campbell-Black returned to England and he dropped Beryl in favour of a renowned actress of the day – Florence Desmond.

In 1934 Tom Campbell-Black ('C B' to his acquaintances) entered the MacRobertson England to Australia air race as co-pilot to Charles Scott. In an age when these pioneer pilots were as well-known as any media star is today, the race attracted world-wide attention. The day before the race the entrants were visited at the start airfield, Mildenhall in Suffolk, by the Royal family (it so happened that Campbell Black had been the King's personal pilot when he visited East Africa a few years previously). Of course, the attention of Royalty only added to the frenzy of public interest in the race.

A Portrait Gallery of Competitors, the Majority of Whom are at Present Likely to Start

Tom Campbell-Black (19) with the entrants for the 1934 MacRobertson Race. Charles Scott is number 18, Jim Mollinson and Amy Johnson are 11 and 12

In 1930 over one million people lined the streets from Croydon to Central London to welcome Amy Johnson back from her record breaking solo flight to Australia

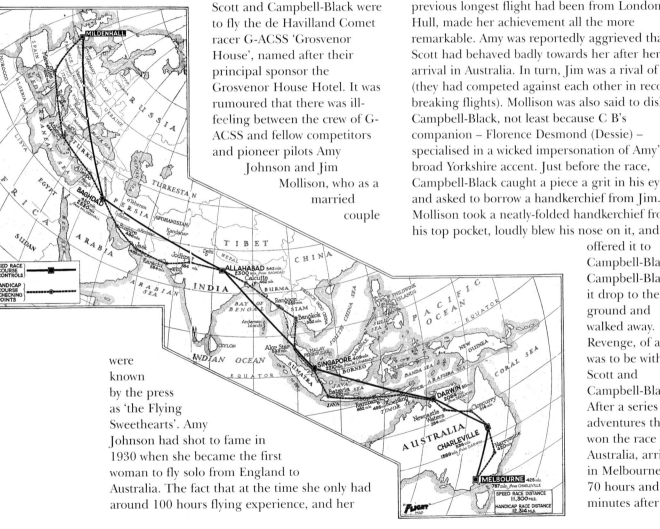

Scott and Campbell-Black were to fly the de Havilland Comet racer G-ACSS 'Grosvenor House', named after their principal sponsor the Grosvenor House Hotel. It was rumoured that there was ill-feeling between the crew of G-ACSS and fellow competitors and pioneer pilots Amy Johnson and Jim Mollison, who as a married couple were known by the press as 'the Flying Sweethearts'. Amy Johnson had shot to fame in 1930 when she became the first woman to fly solo from England to Australia. The fact that at the time she only had around 100 hours flying experience, and her previous longest flight had been from London to Hull, made her achievement all the more remarkable. Amy was reportedly aggrieved that Scott had behaved badly towards her after her arrival in Australia. In turn, Jim was a rival of Scott (they had competed against each other in record-breaking flights). Mollison was also said to dislike Campbell-Black, not least because C B's companion – Florence Desmond (Dessie) – specialised in a wicked impersonation of Amy's broad Yorkshire accent. Just before the race, Campbell-Black caught a piece a grit in his eye and asked to borrow a handkerchief from Jim. Mollison took a neatly-folded handkerchief from his top pocket, loudly blew his nose on it, and offered it to Campbell-Black. Campbell-Black let it drop to the ground and walked away. Revenge, of a sort, was to be with Scott and Campbell-Black. After a series of adventures they won the race to Australia, arriving in Melbourne just 70 hours and 59 minutes after leaving Mildenhall. Amy and Jim retired from the contest in India, the engines of their Comet racer 'Black Magic' over-heated and blown.

On the back of this success, Tom Campbell-Black set his sights on a new goal, the record for the journey from England to the Cape. His first attempt in August 1935, had to be abandoned at Cairo. His next attempt, a month later, ended when (in the laconic words of a 'Flight' report) he and his companion had to leave their Comet racer by parachute, 100 miles north of Khartoum.

In September 1936 Campbell-Black entered the Schlesinger Race to Johannesburg, his mount to be a specially modified Percival Mew Gull G-AEKL. On Saturday 19th September, just two weeks after Beryl Markham had made her record-breaking flight across the Atlantic, he took the Mew Gull to Speke Airport to have it named 'Miss Liverpool', courtesy of his sponsor John Moores of the football pools company. After several flights to show off the aeroplane to the people of Liverpool,

Tom Campbell-Black (centre) with two fellow entrants in the Schlesinger race. This picture was taken just a few days before his death

he finished the demonstration and taxied out from his enclosure to return to London. At the same moment a Hawker Hart, K3044 of 611 (West Lancashire) squadron, was coming in to land after an air-test, flown by Flight Officer P S Slater. In the Mew Gull, Campbell-Black was apparently distracted by something in the cockpit, looking at a map maybe. In the Hawker Hart, Slater was landing directly into the sun, the great bulk of the Hart's Kestrel engine totally obscuring his forward view. There was no air traffic control to give a warning, the onlookers were powerless to intervene. The Hart struck the Mew Gull from behind, smashing the Mew Gull's port wing and undercarriage. The propeller of the Hart tore across the fuselage and into the cockpit. Tom Campbell-Black was mortally wounded. He was rushed to hospital, but died shortly after arriving. In the aftermath of the accident, the wreckage of his Mew Gull was pushed to the nearest building – hangar 1.

A Hawker Hart

Percival Mew Gull G-AEKL
"Miss Liverpool"

THOMAS CAMPBELL BLACK

IT is with the deepest regret that *Flight* records the death, last Saturday, of Mr. Thomas Campbell Black. He was involved in a collision on Speke Aerodrome, Liverpool, between his Mew Gull, which he was to have flown in the South Africa race, and a Service Hart. It appears that, as he taxied out to take off for Gravesend, the airscrew of the slowly moving Hart cut through a wing and into his cockpit, inflicting terrible injuries which quickly proved fatal.

An inquest was opened at Liverpool on Monday but was adjourned for a week.

Tom Campbell Black was born in 1899 and served during the war in the R.N.A.S. and R.A.F. In post-war years, while farming in Kenya, he was a pioneer of civil aviation, and, apart from making thirteen flights between that colony and England, founded Wilson Airways, Ltd. In 1929 he flew from Nairobi to England in eight days. During the visit of the King, then Prince of Wales, to East Africa six years ago, Campbell Black was temporarily appointed his personal pilot. He was also engaged as private pilot to Lord Furness. In 1930 he made the first non-stop flight from Zanzibar to Nairobi, and in the following year rescued Herr Ernst Udet, who was starving on an island in the Upper Nile.

His most notable performance was in the MacRobertson England-Australia Race of 1934, when, as co-pilot with C. W. A. Scott, he gained first place, covering the distance from Mildenhall to Melbourne in 70 hr. 59 min. in a D.H. Comet. Subsequently the Royal Aeronautical Society awarded him the Britannia Trophy for 1934 and the British silver medal for outstanding achievements in aeronautics.

In 1935 he married Miss Florence Desmond, and that August he set out on a Comet to make an attempt on the Cape record, but was forced to abandon the journey at Cairo. During the following month he was off again, in company with Mr. J. H. G. McArthur, on another attempt to lower the record, but, with his companion, was forced to leave the machine by parachute 100 miles north of Khartoum.

In late months he has led British Empire Displays, and the following is a tribute from "J. A. T.," one of his colleagues:

"'C. B.' was not with us all of the time, but each member of the staff looked forward to those long week-ends when he came on tour. The sight of his black-and-silver Puss Moth seemed to signify that all was well with the flying world; his presence was a tonic and an indication that we were going to have a successful week-end.

"Tom Campbell Black was one of the best 'mixers' with whom twenty years of flying has brought me in contact. Rank meant nothing to him, his smile and ready quip were for all. Generous to a fault, he had the happy knack of doing favours that were not recognised as such until long afterwards. The impish seriousness with which he would casually mention a 'sticky' journey, which you knew was more than 'sticky,' endeared him to the hearts of the other pilots. With an unusually good memory, 'C. B.' could keep the party in good humour without in any way usurping the conversation.

"I have a particularly happy memory of him somewhere in the North Country. The proprietor of our hotel had been telling us of the illness of her son, who was to enter the Royal Air Force at Halton in a very short time. The lad's principal distress was that he had been unable to see our show that day, and that he had dearly wanted the autograph of Mr. Black. Someone mentioned the matter to 'C. B.'—and we lost his company for more than an hour. Somewhere there is a boy-mechanic who cherishes not only a famous autograph, but the memory of an hour of talk that encompassed the world.

"It would be intrusiveness on my part to write of Campbell Black's services to aviation, when so many famous pilots in the world will be prepared to pay homage to the master-hand. I need only say that on one occasion I heard him say, 'This field doesn't look too good to me. Let me have a try with two of the staff.' Everyone within hearing moved as one man towards the famous Puss Moth."

The 'Flight' obituary

With just ten days to go before the race to Johannesburg, Amy Johnson announced that if G-AEKL could be repaired in time, she would fly it in the contest. Unfortunately, her motives were questioned, and some thought she was seeking publicity at the expense of Campbell-Black's newly married, now newly widowed, bride – Florence Desmond. In the event, the Mew Gull could not be repaired in time, but the story did not end there. Two years after the crash Amy's husband, Jim Mollison, bought the rebuilt G-AEKL and re-named it 'Southern Cloud'. He offered to loan it to

Amy for a proposed record-breaking flight to rebuild her fortunes, but she declined. With war looming the Mew Gull was hangared at Lympne aerodrome. It was here that the ill-fated machine was destroyed, for good this time, when Stuka dive bombers of the Luftwaffe attacked the airfield in 1940 at the height of the Battle of Britain.

Ill-fortune seemed continued to dog those who had been involved with G-AEKL and Campbell-Black. After their marriage fell apart, both Amy Johnson and Jim Mollison became ferry pilots, using their experience to good effect to deliver military

The re-built G-AEKL at Hatfield during the 1938 Kings Cup air race.
Strangely, the aircraft behind is Comet Racer G-ACSS,
in which Campbell-Black and Scott won the England-Australia race

aircraft around Britain in often appalling weather conditions. On the 5th January 1941, Amy Johnson left Squires Gate airport – Blackpool as it is now – bound for Kidlington airfield near Oxford. The weather was poor with most of the route covered by low cloud. She was flying, appropriately enough, an Oxford twin-engine training aircraft. She never arrived. More than two hours after her ETA at Kidlington, Amy's aircraft crashed into the Thames estuary – 90 miles south east of her intended destination. The crew of a nearby ship reported a parachute, and the captain of the *Haselmere* dived into the icy waters towards a survivor. He was pulled from the water 10 minutes later suffering from exposure, and he died later in hospital. The body of Amy Johnson was never found, and her fate is surrounded by rumour and legend that persists to this day. Eye-witness accounts vary, vital evidence was destroyed and no full enquiry was ever made, despite the fact that the wreckage of Amy Johnson's aircraft lies in just a few metres of water. One of the most persistent rumours is that she was shot down in error by British gunfire although, in all probability, the truth will never be known. In this last truism Amy Johnson has much in common with her American counterpart, Amelia Earhart.

Jim Mollison survived the war, but like many former pioneer pilots he found the relative obscurity of the post-war era difficult to live with. These heroes of their time, once household names the world over, found that they had been replaced by a fresh set of heroes. Military pilots with medals and ribbons, new media darlings, dare devils who could break the sound barrier – these faces and names filled the newspapers instead. Distances that the pioneers risked their lives to cross could be travelled in safety and comfort by anybody who could afford an airline ticket. Today a flight across the Atlantic, or to Africa or to Australia, is no more adventurous than catching a bus. Charles Scott, who won the England to Australia air race with Tom Campbell-Black, committed suicide in 1946 with a bullet to the head. Mollison retreated into drink, a slower form of self-destruction, and died in 1959.

Meanwhile, at Liverpool, the spirit of Tom Campbell-Black seemed to live on. Sightings of a shadowy airman's figure in and around hangar 1 were so frequent that they became an accepted fact amongst those based at Speke. Stories became embellished and blurred over the years, but incidents such as that which Mike experienced in 1970 remained almost common-place.

In 1966 a new main runway for Liverpool airport was built on the banks of the Mersey, to the south of the original airfield. Later an apron and control tower were built alongside and, when the new terminal was opened there in the mid-1980s, the old terminal was closed. As a listed building the original tower and terminal stand deserted, forlorn and boarded-up. If the spirit of Tom Campbell-Black still calls the lift to the basement, no human eyes are there to see it, the noise of its movement goes unheard.

Hangar 1 has seen various uses, not least as an aircraft maintenance area. Late one night an engineer, washing his hands in the toilets of hangar 1 at the end of a late shift, sensed someone watching him, although he believed that he was alone. He whirled round to see a figure in 'old-time flying gear' standing behind him. He bolted from the hangar, leaving the taps running and the lights burning. A security guard, checking hangar 1 in the early hours one morning, found a door unlocked. He checked that the hangar was empty, which it was, and then re-locked the door. Half-an-hour later, he found the same door unlocked again. Still the hangar was empty, so again he re-locked the door and double-checked it. When he found the door unlocked for a third time, he decided that another part of the airfield must need his attention. Another security guard, walking through a dark and empty hangar 1 at night, felt a strong and violent tugging at his sleeve, then his arm was gripped in a powerful grasp. Needless to say, there was nobody alongside him. He fled to the safety of his office where, on rolling-up his sleeve, five bruises – in the pattern of five unseen fingers – were clearly visible on his arm.

A few years ago hangar 1 was closed, its structure giving away to the toll of the weather and years of neglect. Still reports of a shadowy figure in the area persist. A visiting pilot in need of a place to spend the night decided to sleep in an aircraft parked in an adjacent hangar, against the advice of locals. He left at first light the next morning, saying only that he had just had the most unpleasant night of his life. He did not want to discuss what he had seen or heard, nor did he return.

So the legend of 'Captain Black' persists. You have to wonder what it could be that would keep a spirit, if you choose to believe in such things, still roaming the scene of its mortal demise more than half a century ago. Could it be a sense of unfinished business, the Cape record that never was to be his? Could it be the ignominy of being lost in such a needless and unnecessary accident? The official report stated bluntly 'The pilot of the civil aircraft failed to keep a proper lookout when taxying' – an unhappy epitaph for any pilot, let alone someone of Campbell-Black's undoubted skill and experience. For now, light aircraft still pass the spot where Tom Campbell-Black met his end, and a handful of flying schools and privately owned aircraft are still housed in the hangars of the 'old' airfield, in the shadow of the decaying terminal and its abandoned control tower. Once the aeroplanes have gone to the newer 'north' airfield, the future of the site is uncertain. There is a general belief that the buildings will simply be allowed to crumble away, unless a property developer takes a sudden interest in constructing a shopping centre here, or an industrial estate, or some other eyesore.

But whilst the aeroplanes remain, something of grandeur of the 1930s municipal airport lives on too. I revisited the old airfield recently. I wandered around the apron outside the old terminal, I

Hangar 1, 1939

peered through the shattered windows into the gloomy interior of hangar 1. The ghosts of my own past eluded me as surely as the ghost of Captain Black. But this was a warm, sunny day; the noise and bustle of a busy airfield surrounded me. The presence that might have been felt, the uneasiness I remembered in that dark hangar, was not to be found while the sun was still in the sky.

I talked with a flying instructor at one of the schools.

"I'm not sure that I believe in these sightings," he said, "but sometimes, when I'm locking up after night flying, I've felt the hairs at the back of my neck starting to stand up. Then I don't turn around, I just close up quickly and walk away".

I remember that feeling well. The difference is that now, I think I know why. More than 60 years after his death, the legend of one man has somehow outlived that of his fellow pilots who knew greater fame, or lived longer lives. A legend that drew me in, unwillingly almost, and led to the story in front of you.

Rest in peace now, Tom Campbell-Black. You are not forgotten.

The original section of the control tower, RAF Linton-on-Ouse

Epilogue

By early May in 1996, "Ghost Stories of the Air" was almost finished. It only remained to select the photographs and drawings, and send the lot off to the printer. Then I was invited to spend a day at RAF Linton-on-Ouse, and that was a happy chance, because it transpired that two buildings on the airfield – the control tower and the mess – are haunted by a ghost.

Linton was once a famous bomber base, first under No. 4 Group and then No. 6 Group, RCAF. It is now the RAF's No. 1 Flying Training School, and it is where all Britain's combat pilots of the future learn to fly. My visit was fascinating from the start. First, I marvelled at the action on the airfield, with one Tucano trainer lining up for take-off, one pelting down the runway, one climbing away into the distance, and a fourth returning to the circuit on the downwind leg. Between them, the training squadrons must fly over a hundred sorties every day to meet their target. Second, I explored the "dark room" in the tower, where a long row of radar screens show and identify every aircraft in the skies of north-east England. Hit a switch, and you know where that aircraft came from and where it is going. Third, I spent forty minutes in the high-tech apparatus which saves the RAF many costly flying hours by simulating, in a dummy cockpit, everything that can happen to a pilot in the air.

Then came the story of the Linton ghost, which is thought to be the unrequited spirit of Warrant Officer Walter Hodgson, whose Halifax was shot down over Essen on 3rd April 1943, and who spent the rest of World War II in Stalag Luft 3 at Sagan in Silesia, where the "Great Escape" ended so tragically in March 1944. When Hodgson was at last repatriated, he was suffering from tuberculosis – a disease which was to kill him in 1959. He had made it known, in the last days of his life, that he wanted his ashes to be scattered on runway 22 at Linton. That wish was honoured, a commemorative plaque was engraved and erected on the airfield. By the mid-1980s, however, it had become evident that the plaque was being seriously eroded by the wind and weather, and a decision was taken to relocate it under cover. It was mounted in the tower, on the wall which faces the Senior Air Traffic Control Officer's door.

It was shortly after the plaque had been transferred that the misty figure of a tall, well-built man, dressed in a flying suit and wearing a helmet, began to appear, not only in the tower, but also in the mess. One of the first to see "The Ghost of Runway 22", as it came to be known, was Brenda Jenkinson, a pretty fair-haired girl, who was working late one evening in the tower communications room. "He was standing in the corridor," she

Fitters working on a Halifax at Linton-on-Ouse, 1943

said,"when I left the switchboard. About six foot tall, quite broad. I was frightened to death, and I ran back in to say I'd seen a ghost. Later, I wished I'd spoken to him, before he disappeared."

"What would you have said?"

"I'd have asked if I could help him."

The ghost was later seen by Mike Byrne in the radar room, and also by a cleaner in the east wing annexe of the mess. When Squadron Leader Jim Harding, then the SATCO, saw the spectre in his bedroom, he realised that the tales of sightings by his staff had been nothing but the truth. They are still wondering, at Linton, whether they should take the plaque out of the tower, and put it back where it belongs – out there on the airfield, near runway 220.

It only remains to relate, as a postscript, a couple of strange incidents that happened during the writing of the book. I should explain that my modus operandi is to do the rough work, or drafting, in the early evening while sitting in a quiet corner of The George Hotel in Easingwold's market place, occasionally stimulated by some mild intoxicant, and then to try to knock the product into shape on the word processor next morning. The work goes into an electronic file and is temporarily stored in the "random access memory" or RAM, which lies somewhere in the bowels of the computer.

The first odd happening started out like this: I had a letter from David Bannister (who was later to provide many stories for the book), and I noted that he wrote from Warboys. It so happened that I knew the village well from the days when I was based nearby, at RAF Wyton, flying Mosquitoes in the last months of World War II. In answering David's letter, I enquired in passing whether The White Hart, and one of its more congenial patrons, a man called Goldie Everitt, were still going strong.

Two or three days later, I was working on the piece in the chapter that is based on the barmaid's story of the ghostly visitors at her pub, the Hollybush. As the tape recording was indistinct at the point where one of the visitors was asking after village personalities, I used Goldie Everitt's name, which had been in my mind, for the one that she had mentioned. I tapped out the paragraph on the computer keyboard, checked it, and pressed "Enter", at which the passage drifted slowly off the screen. I was surprised, if not to say astounded. I had been using the same"software" for many years, and such a thing had never happened. I typed the paragraph again, and away it went, just as before. I checked the "lay-out", the "tabulation", the "document options" and even resorted to the manual. Nothing helped: that paragraph would not stay where it was put.

Next morning's mail brought David's next letter. The White Hart had burned down, but was to be restored; Goldie Everitt had died soon after the war, leaving a widow and two young children. I sat back and thought the matter over, and I got the message: Goldie was a Warboys man, a White Hart man, the Hollybush had never been his place, and he did not belong there. I went back to the chapter, and tapped out the paragraph, with another name. When I pressed "Enter", everything was normal on the screen. "Sorry about that, Goldie," I said in my thoughts, "I'll be more careful from now on."

The next surprising incident came a few weeks later, the day after I had been working on the

Jack Currie and Senior Air Traffic Controller (SATCO) Andy Radforth outside the Linton control tower, May 1996

chapter about the Canadians. I knew that the story of the Keenans and the ghost of Geoff Monroe was incomplete, and that more research was needed, but I let it lie, and moved on to something else. Next morning, as usual, I "booted up" the computer, logged into the programme, and called up the ghost story file. At that, the software went absolutely crazy. Weird messages came up on the screen: the file was too big, it ought to be broken down into smaller pieces, there was no room in RAM, did I want to retry, ignore, or abort?

I sat staring at the VDU – the visual display unit – for a while, hoping it would settle down and make some sense. Then I tried again, and up came the file, but it was nothing like the file that I had "saved" the day before. That had held over 50,000 words, the whole book up to then – everything I had written in the previous six months; this file held perhaps a fiftieth of that. What remained began with the line: "Quincy, North California. 'He's making my life a misery,' she…"

Again, I got the message. I had not resolved the story of Monroe and the Keenans. I had left the Keenans at their home in Quincy, and in some distress. Monroe did not like that, and he was trying to tell me so. It was just as well, I thought, that from harsh experience I had long followed the practice, as a precaution against electrical failure, accident or theft, of copying a working file from the hard disk onto a "floppy" at the end of every session. For a horrid moment, I feared that Geoff might have fixed the floppy, too, but I put the thought aside. He was, I felt, essentially benevolent: he just wanted me to set his story right.

That afternoon, I talked to Mrs. Sally Pyne, the owner of the hotel where the action all began – something I should have done before. I asked if she had heard from Mrs. Keenan since the ghost had followed her to Quincy. "Yes, I have," she said, "and everything's all right. Geoff has walked into the light." And that was how I wrapped up the story. For The Golden Fleece, however, it was not all over yet.

Sally Pyne went on to tell me that, a year to the day after the Keenans had spent a sleepless night in the hotel, a man and wife from Sunderland, with a twelve-year old daughter, had arrived for a short holiday. On their first day in residence, they had just sat down for lunch when the daughter showed symptoms of unease, and whispered to her mother: "Can we sit somewhere else, Mum?"

"Why, dear? It's nice here by the fire."

The child wriggled, and moved a little closer. "I don't like sitting so close to this little old man."

The mother smiled. "There's nobody there, dear, nobody at all."

The child insisted, and was on the verge of tears. "There is, Mum, and he's sitting beside me. Please, Mum, I don't want to sit here."

The parents exchanged glances, and the woman took her daughter out of the hotel, for a walk along the street known as Pavement, hoping to allay her fears. The father, meanwhile, joked about the matter with Craig, the barman, asking if the place was known for ghosts. "Well," admitted Craig, "we did have one a year ago," and produced a copy of the local paper which recorded the case of Monroe and the Keenans.

The man read the report and, as he did, "his face went whiter and whiter", in the words of Sally Pyne.

"Are you all right?" the barman asked. "Is anything the matter?"

The man put the paper down and stared at the barman. "My name is Keenan," he said. On investigation, it emerged that a small, elderly gentleman, a resident of Walmgate, an ancient access through the city wall, had been an habitu of The Golden Fleece, and had always occupied that same bench-seat by the fire. He had drowned, either by accident or his own intent, in the nearby waters of the River Ouse.

In conclusion, I feel I have the duty to send this message to Keenans everywhere: it may be that the news of Geoff Monroe's transition to a higher plane has been slow to get around the spirit world; so, if you should chance to visit The Golden Fleece in York, you may still have an interesting experience. With that warning, these few stories have to end, but I am sure that there are many more. The ghosts are always out there, somewhere, and they can be with us any time. Happily, none I have written of so far, except for Geoff and Goldie Everitt, has found the need to make corrections or amendments, but I am well aware that there is always time for that.

Contributors:

Mr. David Bannister of Warboys, Cambs;
Mr. Gerald Betts of Bryncoch, W. Glamorgan;
Mr. Reg Cliffe of Bramley, Leeds;
Mr. Dave Daniells of Easingwold;
Trevor Deane of Weston-super-Mare;
Mr. Derek Elkington of Cape Town, South Africa;
Mr. Tony Ellis of Smethwick;
Mr. K.A. Goodchild of Tatsfield near Westerham, Kent;
Lt. Col. Stephen Jenkins, TD, of Wisbech;
Anthony Leicester of Ft Lauderdale, Florida;
Mr. Rex Polendine of Sleaford, Lincs;
The late Mr. Frank Pritchard of Benfleet, Essex;
Mr. Warran I. Quigley of Halifax, Nova Scotia;
Squadron Leaders Andy Radforth and Mike Brooks of RAF Linton-on-Ouse;
Mike Rudkin of Holmes Chapel;
Mr. C. Stephenson-Mole of Islip, Northants;
Mr. T. Stone of Acklam, Middlesborough;
Mr. D.G. Williams of Kempsey, Worcester;

Principal Photographers:

D.F. Daniells
Mark Smith

Drawings:

Lynn Williams

Design:

Wendy Barratt
Rob Taylor of GDi Studio

Glossary and abbreviations

Flak	Anti-aircraft fire
Happy Valley	Bomber Command slang for the Ruhr valley
HCU	Heavy Conversation Unit (converting crews onto the four-engined 'heavy' bombers)
LMF	Lack of Moral Fibre – an official term given to someone unable to continue flying combat missions due to mental stress
Mae West	A lifejacket
MO	Medical Officer
MT	Motor Transport
NCO	Non Commissioned Officer
OC	Officer Commanding
OTU	Operational Training Unit
PFF	Pathfinder Force
PPL	Private Pilot's Licence
Tail-end Charlie	RAF slang for the Rear Gunner
RAF	Royal Air Force
RCAF	Royal Canadian Air Force
RT	Radio Telephony
USAAF	United States Army Air Force
WAAF	Women's Auxiliary Air Force
WT	Wireless Telephone
Watch Tower	Alternative name for control tower, housing Air Traffic Control
Wimpey	Nickname for the Vickers Wellington twin-engined bomber
Window	Strips of metallic foil, dropped in flight to confuse radar
Wop/Ag	Wireless Operator/Air Gunner

Index